Testing the up-ramp for Disneyland's Pirates of the Caribbean at the Arrow Development plant. Ed & Karl are standing at the control panel; Walt Disney is seated in the front row of the boat.

ROLLER COASTERS, FLUMES & FLYING SAUCERS

THE STORY OF ED MORGAN & KARL BACON
RIDE INVENTORS OF THE MODERN AMUSEMENT PARKS.

ROBERT R. REYNOLDS

Northern Lights Publishing

Roller Coasters, Flumes and Flying Saucer
The Story of Ed Morgan and Karl Bacon, Ride Inventors of the Modern Amusement Parks.
Robert R. Reynolds

Published by Northern Lights Publishing
10214 Trailwood Circle
Jupiter, Florida 33478

Cover design by Sandra C. Sallman

Photographs unless otherwise noted are from the collections of Ed Morgan and Karl Bacon. Used by permission.

ISBN 0-9657353-5-4
Library of Congress Catalog Card Number: 98-96860

Publisher's Cataloging-in-Publication
(Provided by Quality books, Inc.)

Reynolds, Robert R. (Robert Ray), 1960-
Roller coasters, flumes & flying saucers : the story of Ed Morgan & Karl Bacon, ride inventors of the modern amusement parks / Robert R. Reynolds. -- 1st ed.
p. cm.
LCCN: 98-96860
ISBN: 0-9657353-5-4

1. Amusement rides--History. 2. Amusement rides equipment industry--History. 3. Morgan, Edgar Allen, 1915- 4. Bacon, Karl. 5. Arrow Development Company. I. Title.

GV1853.2.R49 1999 791'.06'80284
QBI98-1656

FOR
STEPHANIE

CONTENTS

ACKNOWLEDGMENTS

This book could not have happened without the help and abundant support of a number of talented individuals. Special thanks go to Paula and Dana Morgan at D.H. Morgan Manufacturing who believed in this project and went out of their way to coordinate the interviews.

Through the miracle of e-mail I was able to research this book, and eventually meet some extraordinary people. The folks at *The "E" Ticket* magazine provided a valuable research tool in the form of their always interesting publication. They handed me off to Roberta Brubaker at Disneyland who in turn sent me over to Bob Gurr. Bob was a source of much background information, and his stories of Disneyland are always enjoyable.

I also must thank Margaret Adamic at Disney Publishing for letting me search through the Disney Archives. Dave Smith was also extremely helpful, already having the Arrow Development file in hand when I walked in the door.

Many thanks to Ted Crowell for some interesting stories about the installation of "It's a Small World" at the New York World's Fair, and to Dana Hammontree at Knott's Berry Farm for finding some beautiful Corkscrew photographs.

Another e-mail friend, Carol Thornton provided remembrances of growing up around the Arrow Development plant. Her father Ron Toomer also gave much needed insight into the early days of Arrow.

Marty and Maryann Marshall contributed their editing know-how along with a number of comas to the project. Also Mona and

Larry Rogers put the final polish on the manuscript. Many thanks to my wife Laura, who managed to put up with me throughout this entire endeavor.

Finally, I must thank Ed and Karl and their wives and families for allowing me into their homes and lives.

Ed Morgan (left), president of Arrow Development, and Karl Bacon, Vice-President, pose for this photo in the early 1960's.

INTRODUCTION

Who would have thought back in 1946 that a small struggling machine shop named Arrow Development would change the way the world would have fun? In today's setting of themed environments and multimillion dollar attractions, it is hard to picture what the amusement industry was like right after the Second World War. Theme parks did not exist. Kiddielands were popular but small and crude. Larger amusement parks, such as those at Coney Island were becoming a bit ragged and seedy. Valuable raw materials went to war, not to pleasure. What was left after the war was in short supply and extremely expensive.

It was with that background that Ed Morgan and Karl Bacon transformed the technology of amusement. They had help, a dedicated staff and a little boost from a fellow named Walt Disney. But what was perhaps the most important aspect was that Karl's and Ed's talents meshed so well. Karl was the theoretician and was usually a year or two ahead of everyone with his ideas. Ed was the machine guy, able to turn concepts into shippable products. Karl, being soft-spoken, preferred computations to public relations. The latter became more of Ed's job.

Ed's and Karl's accomplishments are indeed stunning when viewed as a whole. Their association with Walt Disney lasted for nearly twenty years and resulted in Arrow having a hand in most every ride system for Disney up until the opening of Walt Disney World. They created dark rides and boat rides, car rides and a group of circling pachyderms named Dumbo. But the most important contribution to Disneyland by Ed and Karl was the Matterhorn Mountain Bobsleds. Before 1959, roller coasters were either wooden or small steel structures built of flat iron rails. The duo decided that to simulate a bobsled, none of these options would work. Instead they came up with an entirely new system, where low slung vehicles would ride on polyurethane wheels over a tubular steel track. The modern roller coaster was born. Today every tubular steel roller coaster in the world can trace its lineage back to Ed and Karl.

That one invention would have sealed Ed and Karl's reputation in the history of the amusement business, but they did not stop there. Karl was fascinated by hydrodynamics and the ability of flowing water to power boats, which eventually led to the flume ride. It was an entirely new type of ride where passengers sat in fiberglass replicas of hollowed out logs, traversing a course and ultimately dropping down a steep hill to a splashy run out. The popularity of the flume ride and it's relative, the hydroflume, made it a must have attraction of virtually every park in the world. Success followed success, as Arrow released the mine train roller coaster to the public. It became the first steel roller coaster that most parks purchased. Later Karl would return to a roller coaster element that had been discarded for sixty years, the loop. Whereas the earlier loops were often violent, even dangerous, Karl's idea was a gentle corkscrew, exciting but safe. The Corkscrew made its debut at Knott's Berry Farm as the first modern looping coaster. Today most looping coasters contain Karl's corkscrew element.

Those three attractions, tubular steel coaster, flume ride and corkscrew, are just part of the amazing career of these two men. Ed and Karl sold the business in 1973 to the Denver and Rio Grande Railroad. Today, after a few other sales and assorted bankruptcies, Arrow Development is now Arrow Dynamics and still in the business of building entertaining rides. If you have ever been to an amusement or theme park, you have probably ridden upon one of Ed and Karl's remarkable creations.

No one is more capable of telling the amazing story of Arrow Development than Ed and Karl. So what follows is the journey, in their own words, from a poor machine shop with one burnt-out truck to a company of 200 employees building attractions for customers throughout the world.

"We'll only have to work three days a week!" Celebrating the 1946 incorporation of Arrow Development. (From left: Ed and Betty Morgan, Angus and Phyllis Anderson, Karl and Jane Bacon, Bill and Evie Hardiman.)

EARLY DAYS

Precocious is a word that can be applied to both Ed and Karl in their formative years. Adept at using tools, and with creative minds, it was not difficult for them to perceive the possibility of combining everyday objects into unique ride systems. The future inventors of trend-setting attractions started their adventures early in life, as Ed's childhood memories show:

Ed: When I was fourteen, using the motor from my mothers washing machine, and about 200-feet of extension cord from my fathers supply, I motorized a coaster wagon. One might say the result was an "electric car" with a very short range, limited only by the length of the cord, and my parents patience.

I spent the following summer building, then "perfecting" a small car using a wooden frame with small wire wheels shod with bike tires and powered with a commercial lawn mower engine. Unfortunately, on my first trip around the block, I met our town's motorcycle cop and had to put it away until I got a license.

My father was a building contractor and had a four car garage on the back of our lot, with an apartment above it. The garage space was used for storage of building materials and tools, a treasure trove for projects. The summer I was sixteen, my father was out of town on a job, and my brother and I and a couple of friends needed a summer project. Someone suggested we build a roller coaster. It seemed like a good idea at the time, and our lot was ideal, in that it was very deep from the street in front to the alley in back. Demonstrating a total lack of planning, we started out with an eight foot folding step ladder. The first drop started at the top of the ladder. The track bed was of 1x12 inch pine with side boards nailed to it. The coaster car was a short plank supported by four roller skates modified for this purpose.

In operation, we pulled the car to the top of the ladder, climbed in, and took off. Great fun, but think of how much better it would be if it were higher and longer! The next step was to add 2x4 inch legged supports progressively higher up. We saw right away that they were unstable, and had to add diagonal bracing. We were learning fast, but not fast enough to sit down and plan and consider the consequences.

This stage, when finished, required an extension ladder to reach the top. It provided a fast ride — too fast at the end of the track. Our solution to this was to add track with a small hill.

In some ways I am reminded of stories I have read of the trials and tribulations of early coaster builders. Our next step was to add a few more taller supports, and eventually tie the track to the roof of the second story apartment. We then laid track on the roof slope to the ridge. We now had a zinger of a coaster, from the alley to the street. To scrub off speed at the end, we dug two post holes for 4x4 inch posts and stretched truck inner tubes over them, providing a cushioned stop with a rebound as a bonus.

Unfortunately, one of my friends was horsing around and rocking the car. About half way down he derailed it and broke his collar bone. This ended the coaster episode. My father made sure of that!

Karl: I recall the time when I was in my third year of high school and I was extremely interested in chemistry. I tried a number of experiments with explosives and gun powders. One evening in the kitchen I had the hydrogen generator going, but when the chemicals got low, the flame crept up into the generator and blew up the flask sending glass all over the room. Luckily no one was seriously injured, but it so startled my grandmother that she cut her hand on the glass. Obviously I was forbidden to ever do experiments in the house again!

Later, I did try my experiments in the bunk house. It was called the bunk house because the three of us boys slept in one of its two rooms. This was before electricity had arrived at our farm, so I had a Coleman lantern up by a window. I had just finished with an explosive, and I had read where it was very sensitive to handle when dry. I had a black substance on a wet filter paper, which I placed by the window to dry. In a few minutes, there was a loud bang, which broke the window and lantern. After that, I was told to stop making explosives period!

While being naturally mechanically inclined, it took a major world event to shape the careers of these two men and bring them together to start a company that would change outdoor entertainment forever.

Ed: At the beginning of World War II, I was prime canon fodder. I knew I would be drafted and I wasn't anxious to do that. So my brother and I went and enlisted in the Army Air Corps. I passed the vision test and the physicals and all that. I was at the top end of the age for cadets. My brother was two years younger so he went pretty soon. He went through basic training and came out as a second lieutenant in the Army Air Corps. They shipped him out to the South Pacific, which he never came back from. I was told then that even though I was in the Army Air Corps, unless I got into essential industry, I could still be reclassified. I applied at Hendy Iron Works; actually it was Hendy Westinghouse, it was a Navy plant. What we made were torpedo launchers with five tubes. They were twenty-one inch diameter tubes that they put the torpedo in with a charge of gunpowder. It comes out the nozzle at sixty miles an hour. I spent the war years there, and that's where I met Karl.

When I went to work there, they asked me if I was a machinist, and though I had done some machine work before, I didn't consider myself to be a machinist. They said, "Well, we have a lot of openings for machinists now; would you be willing to go to work as a machinist helper?" I had a need to get under their umbrella, so naturally I said yes. I went to work as a machinist helper, and I worked under a guy that was an egomaniac. He was kind of a flake, actually. He left me to do pretty much my own thing. I began to get involved in jobs that were well beyond the helper scope. Before very long I ended up designing and supervising the testing facility. Remember, these things were leaving the breach at 60 miles per hour and we were shooting them into a wooden trough that's tapered and catching them at the end, squeezing them and catching them with a big hydraulic ram. I think Karl got involved in the hydraulic ram end of things.

I was out on the test platform one day and a torpedo came tearing down the trough. They had a piano wire that ran out a hole in the breach, and it was on a reel that determined muzzle velocity. That wire was too small to see, really. I felt it sting my cheek, and all of a sudden my finger hurt. I looked down and the wire was sticking

Workers at the Hendy Plant standing in front of torpedo launchers. Karl is third from left in the first standing row.

through my finger. So I pulled it out and it has black gunpowder all over it. Kind of an unsatisfactory event.

Karl and I were involved in a number of projects there. We were involved in a prototype jet engine. We also started producing the rockets for the Iwo Jima invasion. I was under so much pressure, and I had a brother that was out there in that theater too. Then they restricted my hours. So what I would do is go out the gate, punch out, and sneak back in. A lot of times, I didn't come home at night. I didn't do that every day, naturally, but I would have something going that needed to be brought to fruition and I couldn't stand being separated from it.

Karl: I too didn't want to be a foot soldier; so I went to the Presidio in San Francisco and took an all day exam for radar, which I passed, and I was offered two years at either Stockton or Salinas Jr. College. In the meantime, Hendy got another deferment for me. I was then Head of Machine Tool Maintenance in the Navy Plant. So I tore up the papers and went back to work.

Hendy was a beautiful plant with brand new machinery. But at the end of the war there was a strike at Hendy and we got tired of it.

Ed: They put us on the picket line and we got tired of that!

Karl: So we decided to start our own business. That was about 1946. We met with an attorney in town, and he asked what the name of our business would be. Ed looked down at his tie and he had a stickpin. Ed said, "Arrow." The name stuck.

Ed: Well, the attorney said, "That's good; it puts you at the front of the phone book."

Karl: He asked us what our business was going to be, and we didn't know. Fabrication and machine work was all we knew at the start. Ed and I built our first shop. We laid the brick ourselves, built the whole thing. Our first job was a test run-out furnace for the Navy.

Ed: We made a set of rolls before we did that job. The furnace had concentric shells on it for insulation and it was fired with natural gas inside. That heated a jet engine rotor up. We had no way to roll the sheet metal and we didn't have the money to have it done, so we took scrap steel and a torch. We cut pieces and made the rolls so we could make the parts to make the run-out furnace.

Karl: Ed and I took our money and we went to Los Angeles to buy an old worn-out lathe and mill for the shop. We stayed at a flop house for $2.00 a night. We couldn't afford anything better.

Ed: Karl, I don't tell people that, but you're right! Do you remember all night long the boozers in the alley down below were whooping and hollering and we couldn't sleep? I think that's where Karl came up with the expression that "poor folk have poor ways."

Karl: Once we were coming home to the hotel, such as it was, and a man walked up to us. I hadn't shaved since the day before. He said, "Could I trouble you for a dime?" I told him we didn't have anything to spare. He said, "Take this newspaper and maybe it will help you!" We were poor!

Ed: What little money we had, we had to husband quite closely because we had to somehow keep going.

After the end of World War II there were no vehicles available of any kind. As far as a truck was concerned, they were like gold. There were no price controls or anything, they all came off at the end of the war. I had an acquaintance at an auto wrecker and I called and asked them if they had any trucks. He said, "We've got a pretty good one here that belonged to Stockton Feed and Fuel, but it was in a fire. The tires are burned and cab scorched, but we could sell you that." So we bought this thing, and dragged it home and took all the charred wood and metal off it, and restored it up to a point. Then we needed to start using it. There was no padding on the seat springs, just burlap.

Karl: We also did work for Stanford Linear Accelerator, and for a crop duster company.

Ed: Then the crop dusting business went bankrupt. That was our main business at that time. When they went bankrupt it left us. . .

Karl: High and dry.

Ed: The materials that were made, and the materials that were on route were not worth anything. We were really scrambling for work.

Arrow's first, and slightly singed truck, with their first product; a test run-out furnace for the Navy.

Karl: Ed and I washed our faces, put on clean shirts and went to Dura Bond Bearing Company, and asked Jack Fowle for a loan of $5,000 and he said, "No, But I will give you an order for $5,000 worth of work." That solved the problem for awhile. The work entailed both welding and machine work.

Then we started doing work for Hewlett Packard.

Ed: The way HP usually worked was if they were buried or had problems that they really didn't want to face, they'd give it to us. When we got things going well, they'd take it back and do the manufacturing themselves and keep it in house.

Karl: We made everything.

Ed: Karl was right down to the nitty gritty on these tiny electronic assemblies. When it came to fruition, and it all worked, then HP took it back. After awhile we learned it was a cycling sort of thing. But they kept bringing us new ones all the time.

Karl: One man walked into the shop and said, "I hear you boys do most anything here." I said, "We try to." He said, "I've got a little problem." And he pulled out his false teeth and said, "I'd like to grind a little off here." I said, "The grinder is over there. Do it yourself!"

Ed: Another time, a guy came in and wanted us to develop a sprinkler. It turned out he was terminal with cancer and he wanted us to develop this thing before he died. We just couldn't because we were really buried right then. He said, "This project has to be finished before I die, and the doctor says I'm going to die in so many days." We hated to say no to the guy.

Karl: One day we had a fire. We went down there and the fire department had gotten there before us. To put the thing out, one of the firemen was breaking out all the windows, and I yelled at him to stop.

Ed: We were machining magnesium.

Karl: The magnesium was in fifty gallon barrels. Someone tried to put a cover over it and put it out but the heat was too much for him. The fire went up twenty feet and set the ceiling on fire.

Ed: Magnesium is wicked stuff, and it was fine chips from a milling machine. Dry magnesium chips, and when it caught on fire, it was like a rocket. We had a mansard roof and then there are windows and a roof above that. This guy was on top of the roof and he was a big guy. He was kicking the windows out with his boots. Boom, crash, boom, crash and Karl was trying to get him to stop before he ruined our whole building. It was a real long building with lots of windows to go yet.

LIL' BELLE

Karl: Eventually, we got started in the amusement business. We noticed in the paper that they were taking bids for a twenty-foot merry-go-round ride, and auto ride, for Alum Rock Park in San Jose. We sent Bill Hardiman down there to get a copy of the bids.

Ed: I think what happened there was that the first ad that I noticed was for playground apparatus. We did bid on it and we did get some of that work. We built playground apparatus for the schools in San Jose. Then the second time was for the carousel.

Karl: For the carousel, we sent to Allan Herschell and got their price on a twenty-foot merry-go-round because we didn't know what those things cost. We bid it less freight from New York to California, and we got the job! Then they decided we were too small, and we had to post a bond to do the work. We knew nothing about merry-go-rounds at that time. But we did know a fellow at a carnival in Palo Alto.

Ed: He was very well known in the carnival business.

Karl: We went to see one of his merry-go-rounds, and measure the shaft and gears to see how the thing worked. We came back to Arrow and built one. We built it out of steel.

Ed: Everything had been wood up until then. This was the first of the all steel carousels. Incidentally, the machine that we measured was a big machine, so we had to scale it down because the one that the park in San Jose bought was a small machine, only a 20-footer. We had to extrapolate that and scale it down to the size we were building.

Karl: Ed and I once took a 20-foot carousel to Salem, Oregon in the summer on a flat bed truck. The truck had been through a fire and we had rebuilt it, but the front seat just had shop rags thrown over the springs. There weren't any floorboards. Not even a floor mat! We got there about midnight and set the merry-go-round up. Then we looked for a place to stay. We didn't realize it, but with the fair on there were no vacancies. So we headed for Albany, about 25 miles south. We got to the bottom of the grade and ran out of gas. We had to spend the night with the truck, so I got on the springs in the front seat and Ed got on a packing crate in the back.

An early Arrow Development merry-go-round. A twenty-foot diameter machine could be purchased from Arrow for $4,800 in 1949.

Cold! My God. Four o'clock in the morning we woke up cold, miserable and hungry.

Ed: The reason we ran out of gas was that there were no gas stations open. We were hoping to get to Albany before we ran out of gas, but we didn't make it. Being a fair, it had to be up and operating the following morning, so we had no choice but to keep working until it was set up. By that time, of course, all the gas stations were closed, and everything else. Karl remembers things that I had forgotten; maybe I prefer to.

Karl: About that time, there was a forty-foot merry-go-round that a fellow in Washington bought, and it had to go there. We worked all night loading it. It was heavy! We had to carry the shaft, the horses, and everything out.

Ed: The people who bought it were very well known in the Seattle area. They had a big carousel concession in the city park.

Karl: In 1952, we sold a 45-foot merry-go-round to a park in Fresno. We had to set it up and install it. We took some men with us but we were short of money. We could put them up in a hotel, but we slept outside. We wrapped ourselves in the merry-go-round's canvas top and spent the night.

Ed : We bought them an awful lot of hamburgers.

In the early days we made cast aluminum horses, but during the Korean War they could not allow us an allotment of aluminum. They didn't know how much the war was going to escalate. So we shifted to magnesium to make carousel horses and they let us do that. What we found out is that with magnesium horses, after we welded them, when they chilled they would crack. We had to build an oven to put the horses in so they wouldn't crack. We were really in a rush to deliver these horses, and it was a temporary oven without very good

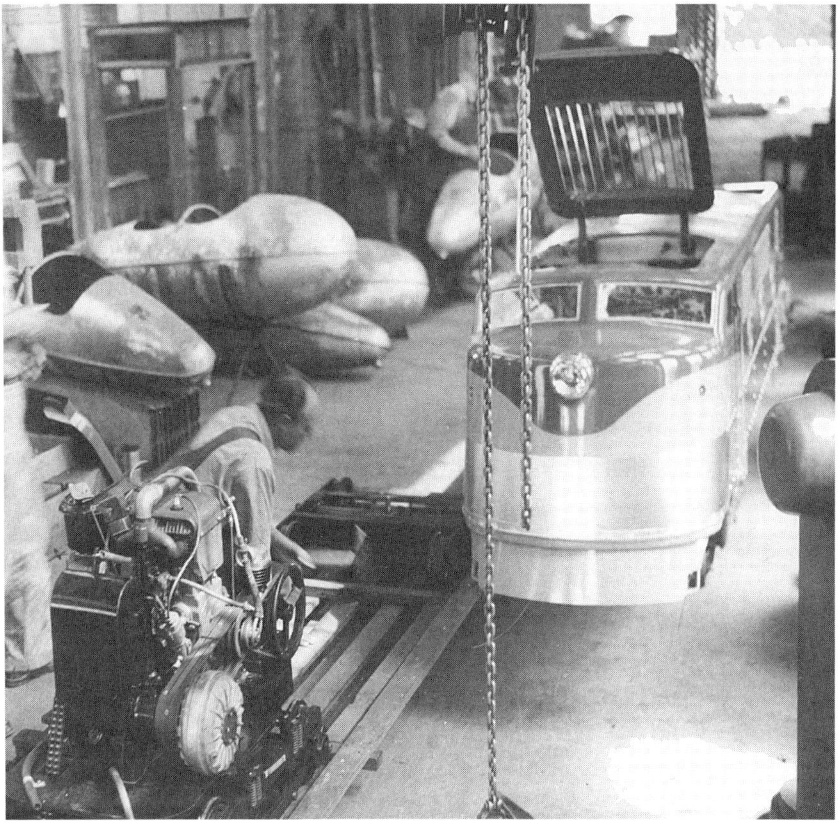

Inside the Arrow plant a train nears completion while war surplus fuel tanks are being made into ride carriages for a simple rotating ride.

heat control. One of the guys reached in there and grabbed a horse by the hoof, with tongs, and when he pulled it out he just had the leg. No horse! So he reached in and grabbed another leg, and that one came off.

We mostly made portable carousels, and portables are plain because most of the baroque crestings were plaster, and you can't have that on a portable. Now they're fiberglass. They'd tear these things down after three or four days and move on so everything had to be extremely portable. They were, from the mechanical standpoint, very advanced. But from the esthetic standpoint, I am really ashamed of them in that respect.

Another ride, we made out of war surplus fuel tanks from airplanes. You could buy them for ten bucks each or something like that. You couldn't create anything like it for a pile of money. They came in crates so they weren't all beat up. We bought dozens and dozens of them. We had templates where you could cut a well out of them and put seats in them. We suspended them and made little rocket ship rides out of them. It was an inexpensive ride and we sold lots of them.

We also did a lot of train rides. They all start from sheet metal sheets, and are all hand made. Karl calculated the gear set, and machined the entire box for each train. The wheels of course are cast, and the drive mechanisms are all fabricated separately. On the eight-wheel drives, there's a drive shaft that goes to the back truck. That is for a situation where you have heavy hills you need to climb. We got a lot of pleasure out of those, because they gave a lot of pleasure. We sold one to the city of Fresno, and it had been operating for a couple of weeks. The Rotary Club had financed it, so the Rotarians were out there operating it. They turned it over to the Rotary people without telling them very much on how to operate it. So some guy flipped the switch while the train was still on it. That took the back

Plug and mold for a carousel horse.

The simple merry-go-round pictured above was perfect for small fairs and parks. The miniature trains below mimicked the aerodynamic look of the modern diesel locomotive.

coach off on it's own; it jumped the track and split the coupling. Here this thing was plowing a track across a field all by itself! It was lucky it didn't tip over and spill everybody. We advised them to put interlocks on all the switches so that only trained personnel could release the interlocks.

Karl: We got a contract with the city of Oakland to put rides in a park out at Lake Merritt. So we formed a little company called Easbey, separate from Arrow. We also made a boat ride for the estuary out at Lake Merritt.

Ed: That was Lil' Belle. It was powered by a paddle wheel in the back and a small gasoline engine in the front under a housing. It was a real paddle wheeler. The hull was a flotation hull, with two separate compartments that were sealed so nothing could happen to ever cause it to sink or capsize.

Lil' Belle, the little craft that started Arrow's association with Disney.

Karl: Before we put the superstructure on it, we tried it out.

Ed: Yeah, we decided we needed a longer, better run than we were able to get in small lakes. So we got some tide tables, and we took it to San Mateo and we launched it with the tide. It was nighttime, and we did this purposely, because they wouldn't have given us permission.

Karl: We almost ran into a sailboat. A fellow came out and was madder than the devil.

Ed: We went out past the breakwater, out on the bay, and we were having a ball. Then we suddenly realized that the swells were growing and it changed pretty fast. After awhile we were pretty close to shipping water over the bow. It wasn't intended for the ocean so we nearly swamped it. About that time somebody in the yacht harbor turned on a spotlight and picked us out. Pretty soon after that, there was a patrol boat on our case. They just gave us what for!

The day that Lil' Belle was inaugurated, the mayor was there and we discovered a mud ridge on the bottom of the estuary that we didn't know about. We slid gently up on it and there it was. The paddle wheel was running like mad and we weren't going anywhere.

Incidentally, we thought we invented something new on this boat. One thing we didn't anticipate is that they get some pretty good winds up there. We found in some cases you couldn't keep from being pushed over to the banks. So we put little hydraulic motors underneath with propellers on them that were ninety degrees to the hull, fore and aft. By touching the control on those, if the wind was blowing you sideways, you could keep the boat from being pushed. It also saved time in docking. Shortly after that, I was in Europe taking a ride up the Rhine, and I discovered that they've been doing that for a long, long time! Nothing new about it.

Lil' Belle takes to the water at Lake Merritt in Oakland, California.

Lil' Belle was really how we got acquainted with the Disney organization. A big customer of ours went bankrupt, an aircraft company in Kansas, and they left us scrambling. We put all of our eggs in one basket. We were making really fine dusting equipment for Luscombe Cropster Airplanes. The airplane was originally designed for spotting troops. It was a high wing, slow speed aircraft that was absolutely ideal for dusting. They were developing the aircraft for that, and we were making equipment for it. They went bankrupt, and we were scrambling, and two things happened.

I read in the newspaper about Disneyland. We were operating Lil' Belle in Oakland. We thought, boy here's a chance to get in on

MERRY GO ROUNDS TRAINS

ARROW DEVELOPMENT CO.

AUTO RIDES PLANE RIDES

243 MOFFETT BOULEVARD, MOUNTAIN VIEW CALIFORNIA

January 6,1953

Mr.Richard Irvine,
W.E.D.Enterprises,
2400 West Alameda Ave.,
Burbank,Calif.

Dear Sir:

Thank you for your inquiry on our stern wheeler boat. I regret that we do not have the photographs and information on it worked up as yet . However we are having these things prepared and will forward some to you as soon as they are completed.

We were quite pleased with the amount of interest shown in this boat even though the pictures we showed at the convention were very sketchy. This early interest caught us a little unprepared as we had not planned on releasing the advertising on it for another month. We are rushing it through,though,and you should have your copies very shortly.

Very truly yours,

ARROW DEVELOPMENT CO.,INC.

by Wm.J.Hardiman

The first communication from Arrow to Disney, following shortly after a request by Dick Irvine for information on the Lil' Belle.

this thing. The newspapers were very sketchy as to what Walt Disney was going to do. But they did respond. This excited us so much that we got permission from the city of Oakland to dry-dock the boat, truck it down, wash it, polish the brass and put it on a stand.

They came to look. They walked right by it and they didn't even slow down. Talk about a sinking feeling! I had no idea as to the scope of Disneyland. Of course there is a great bit of difference between our boat and the boat they would build for Disneyland. No one had heard of a theme park at that time. That was the introduction.

They talked to us there, and they saw some of the little vehicles that we were building, and Walt Disney came along and looked. I saw him look to some of his people and nod. At least he saw something that didn't displease him.

It wasn't too long after that, they asked us about Mr. Toad. I hand-built one car. They came and looked at it, and they didn't ask for too much change. We just went from the original sketch by Bruce

The Flying Platform gave the rider of the 1950's the thrill of personal flight.

The 30" gauge train was popular for it's beauty. A 48 HP Ford Industrial Engine was hidden in the coal car and powered the attraction.

Bushman. No drawings were ever made of the car. Not a single drawing. I lofted one, and when that was lofted I took templates from it, and from the templates we built the subsequent ones. With the templates, we were able to cut out the sheet metal parts. The templates, which were cut out of plywood, showed the line of the fender and the line of the hood. We went directly from a hand made prototype to templates and to the parts. That was the big difference between us and Disney. Everything they did was superb. Their welders were artists. They could write a book on the subject. Everything they turned out was like that. There were times we did things just because it was necessary for survival. Poor folk have poor ways.

Mr. Toad would become a favorite Disneyland attraction and the start of a relationship between Arrow and the Disney organization that would last nearly twenty years. The twelve toad vehicles, with such names as Winky, Ratty and Weasel propelled nearly 700 guests an hour through a tight weaving course. The attraction simulated a collision with a train and a subsequent ride through hell that made it one of the darker of the dark rides.

After a major refit in the early eighties, the cars now travel through a larger and more elaborate toad hall. The early metal vehicles themselves have since been replaced with fiberglass replicas. The attraction is dearly loved by many, as was witnessed by the controversy surrounding the closing of the Walt Disney World version in favor of a Winnie the Pooh ride. Ed Morgan's contribution to this ride can not be overstated, nor the transforming power of Disney to move a small machine shop in entirely new directions.

The purpose of any amusement attraction is to bring a smile to the face of the rider. By this standard, even the most basic of the early Arrow Development ride systems succeeded. The talented and perfection driven Disney organization was about to force Arrow into becoming much more sophisticated in the art of fun.

Walt Disney inspecting the car that would land Ed and Karl the job of creating Disneyland's Mr. Toad vehicles. (from left: Walter Schulze, Karl Bacon, Dick Irvine, Joe Fowler, Ed Morgan, Walt Disney)

BUILDING DISNEYLAND

Disneyland would be the catalyst in the transition of Arrow Development from a machine shop that, while an amusement supplier, was still multitasked and willing to take on any work in order to survive, to a full-fledged ride manufacturer. It would also begin a relationship between Arrow and Disney that would last for twenty years. During that period, Arrow Development would be responsible for building almost every ride system to enter Disneyland and later Walt Disney World.

The amount of work given to Arrow at the beginning of Disneyland's construction must have been daunting for a small shop. In addition to the Mr. Toad vehicles and track, they were also responsible for the Tea Cup ride, Dumbo the Flying Elephants, King Arthur Carousel, Casey Jr. and Snow White.

Although Disneyland was the dream and vision of Walt Disney, many others helped to bring that dream to reality. Joe Fowler was in charge of construction and was one of the main contacts between Disney and Arrow. Formerly a Navy Admiral, he was still often referred to by that title. Richard Irvine, an art director for many years with Disney, headed up the design team for Disneyland and later ran WED Enterprises, the design arm of the Disney organization. Vic Greene and Bruce Bushman, both art directors, were responsible for many of the early design elements at Disneyland. Both were involved closely with Arrow in bringing sketches to life as three-dimensional attractions. Roger Broggie was head of Disney's machine shop and a fan of railroads. He was responsible for helping Walt

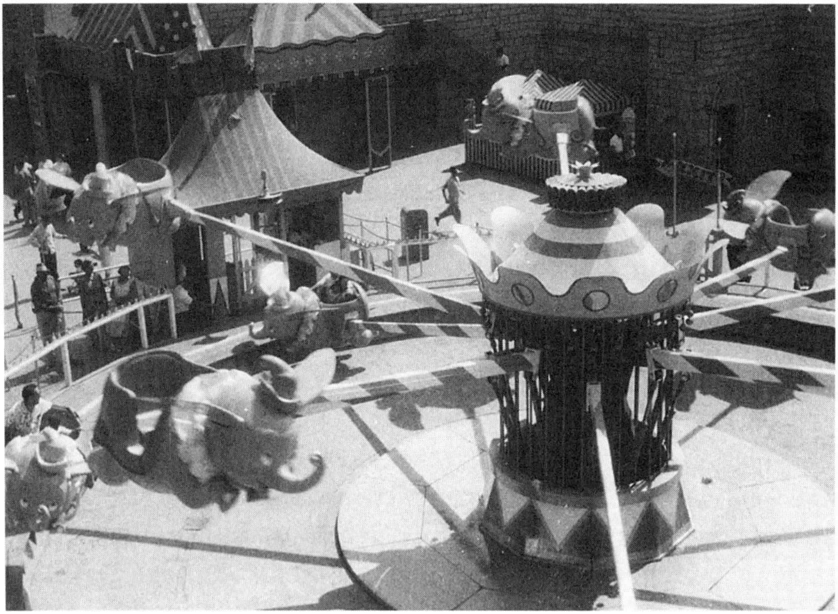

Milking the Elephants. Technological problems almost grounded the flying pachyderms.

Disney set up his own miniature train system in the backyard of his Holmby Hills home. These people were among the core group that brought Walt Disney's concept of a new kind of amusement park into being. They also maintained a close working relationship with Ed and Karl as plans for Disneyland developed into working ride systems.

Disneyland opened on July 17th, 1955 for the then astronomical sum of $17 million dollars. The Arrow built ride systems to debut on opening day were: Mr. Toad's Wild Ride, Snow White's Adventures, the Mad Tea Party and the King Arthur Carousel. The Casey Jr. Circus Train was phased in on July 31st and Dumbo Flying Elephants on August 16th of 1955.

Despite the best efforts of all involved, not everything went perfectly on opening day. Other than the 1922 King Arthur Carousel, all the attractions were prototypes, systems never before attempted. Through experimentation by Arrow and the Disney staff over the following months, and with a great deal of trial and error, the rides would finally be running consistently and reliably.

Karl: Disney gave us so much work that we couldn't do it all; we were too small. So we hired an engineer to help us with Dumbo. He used these free surface accumulators on the ride, one for each elephant. But they would get out of balance, since there was no piston to separate the oil from the nitrogen. The nitrogen would get into the system and screw it all up. Later on I added the pistons in each cylinder to stop the sickening motion.

Ed: Karl called it shaving cream. The guy's idea was clever and we didn't have enough experience to gainsay it. His idea was that you could cut the horsepower that it took to lift the elephants way down by putting oil under the pressure of nitrogen, and that took the static weight. All you had to lift was the small differential. It was a wonderful idea, but he didn't know that in order to do that, you had to have a piston that separated the gas from the oil. So what happened was that the rapid movement of the oil would mix the nitrogen and the oil and make foam. The foam threw the whole thing out of stability and it was too late to change it.

An Arrow Development Snow White vehicle exits the show area.

Two of the Arrow Development staff take a break in an unfinished Snow White vehicle.

Karl: We used a fellow by the name of Paul Harvey on site. We left him down thereto...

Ed: . . .milk the Elephants!

Karl: While they were loading, he'd go out there and drain the system and put in clean oil. We elected him. I went back with a drawing to build a replacement manifold for the ride.

Ed: He was a wonderful employee, and we just left him there on opening day. It was a mean thing to do. They were actually operating the ride, and he was in the inner enclosure. He's draining fluid and putting fluid back in between time of load and unload. Disney was insistent that the ride would run because they had so many problems in the early days. We went along with it, so we left Paul there while we went home to build a manifold and everything that went with it. At that time we couldn't get new pumps in a hurry, so we were going to military surplus stores. We were buying hydraulic pumps from aircraft servo systems, because there was no way we could order and get pumps in time to keep this thing going and not have egg on our face and Disney's also. We knew that it was all throw-away, that it all had to be redone, but on an interim basis, with the new manifolding and the war surplus pumps, we made the ride work. We saved Disney's, and our image but at a very great cost in effort and dollars. We were running back and forth to the surplus store until ten at night.

Karl: We worked all night long. Bill Hardiman, a former partner, and I would visit Paley Supply until ten or eleven at night.

Ed: We had the use of Disney's machine shops too.

Karl: Opening day was a nightmare.

Ed: Art Linkletter remembered that day as well. Art Linkletter was walking backwards with a mike and the TV cables were all over the place. Linkletter got tangled up in the cables and went down. So on TV, Linkletter is talking and all of a sudden there's a blank. He was lying on his back on the pavement.

King Arthur's Carousel started out as a 1922 Dentzel menagerie and was converted by Arrow to 85 horses.

ED: We also had a problem with the Snow White cars. They had three wheels, two in the back, one in front. This allowed you to go around very sharp corners. Those cars have a little step. It wasn't intended as a step. They gave us sketches for the shells, and we did the machinery to fit inside the shells that we made. The shell had, behind the back seat, a kind of ledge on it. What happened was that the operating people, when it came into the station, discovered that ledge. They would jump on it and ride the cars into the station from the last door as they came out of the dark. The heavy guys would, with the leverage of their weight, lift the front end off the track. So the carriage that steered the thing was now running loose. We didn't know what was going on. We were off doing other things, and we come back, and they were having all these problems. We discovered that these kids were jumping on, and they didn't know what they were doing, of course. They were derailing all the cars. In the mean time, they wrecked the carriages on some of them, due to the impacting on the pavement. So some had to be taken off and put in the alcove, and the ride run on a minimum basis.

Disney had also made all of the inside doors operate by air cylinders. Karl, do you remember… ?

Karl: I sure do. They kept adding cylinders until they pulled the doors off!

Ed: Disney used Stanley hinges, regular door hinges of all things, in something like that. Just like your house door hinges. The cylinders were mounted real close to the hinge point. It turned out that the cylinders were not strong enough to open the doors fast enough so the cars wouldn't hit them. They rushed up town and bought surplus cylinders and kept adding them to the doors. They finally got enough power that they were uprooting all the hinges, and the doors were falling onto the track!

King Arthur's Carousel was another Arrow project. Unlike their custom built merry-go-rounds, the Disneyland machine was a preexisting carousel that was modified to fit the new park's needs. Originally, King Arthur's Carousel started as a three row, 72-animal, menagerie Dentzel from 1922. Its first home was Sunnyside Park, Toronto, Canada.

Disney thought that galloping horses would be more fitting for an Arthurian Carousel than menagerie animals, and Arrow needed to come up with a number of horses as replacements. Two other carousels gave up their horses so that the Dentzel became a four-row, 85-horse machine.

Ed: We also did King Arthur's Carousel. It was built around 1922, or something like that.

Karl: In the early fifties, when we would finish a ride such as a carousel, we would invite all the ladies and kids down to ride the prototype. I remember one time when my oldest daughter Susan was riding a horse about ten in the evening, sound asleep with her hands clasped around the horse pole!

Casey Jr., the little engine that could... and did!

Ed: Typically, Walt Disney would come to the plant and he'd look at something. The Casey Jr. train was the second thing we did for them. The first was Mr. Toad. We mocked up the engine, and it was a lot of work because of all the oddball shapes that you're not used to. We thought it was great. Disney came, and he looked at it and walked around and looked again. Then he's over in the corner talking to the art director, Vic Greene. Vic comes over and says, "Walt thinks that if you fatten the boiler up just a little bit it might give it a little more feeling." And then he'd say, "Walt thinks that the steam chests, if they were just tipped a little more… " So what it amounts to is that by the time they'd leave, I'd be thinking, my God, we've been working our butts off, and really there's nothing here that we can use. You just can't make the boiler over, so you start with another engine next to it and build it up. But I was told by Roger Broggie somewhere along that time, "Well you better get used to it, because that's the way it's going to be if you work with movie people. . ." He looks around to see if anyone was listening, ". . . and particularly with art directors."

Karl: I remember the problem we had with Casey Jr. climbing the hill. From the drive wheel it went to sprockets, and the sprockets engaged a chain. Without that you couldn't have enough friction in the world to go up that hill.

Ed: It was essentially a cog drive system. On opening day, the guy with the bulgy eyes, Jerry Colonna, was supposed to drive the train, but he chickened out. So they put his clothes on Karl and Karl was the driver for opening day. Karl had a lot of guts. Colonna just chickened out. He looked at that hill and said, "No!"

Ed: Walt Disney would sometimes come to the shop and we used to go to lunch with him. Walt never brought any money with him. He'd look at Vic Greene or Bruce Bushman and ask if they had any money. He knew they did. They better have!

Another time we were at the studio in Burbank. We were there early one morning for a meeting and I was looking out the window. Walt Disney drives up in an old beat up Cadillac convertible with a tattered top on it. He gets out. He had a bathrobe on and pajamas on under it.

Karl: He also had slippers on.

Ed: He comes in and lies down on the floor. Walt stretches out and puts his hands under his head. He's asking questions and conducting this meeting. So he was pretty informal.

Karl: I lay down on the floor beside him and was explaining things to him!

Ed: On one hand the Disney organization was so hospitable, then they'd miss out on the little details. While we were on construction, I'd go down there and I couldn't get in because nobody had cleared me at the gate. These security guys are calling and they can't reach this guy and they can't reach that guy. Finally, I have to get to work so I go and pay my way in. I know where all the back gates are, so I open a gate and go where I'm supposed to go. So I thought, I'm going to fix these guys. When I got back I told Walt Shulze to bill Disney for my entry fee. Really make it obvious. Well, that changed things for awhile. Then the same old thing started happening. I had to pay to go to work!

Karl: We had a fixed bid on all the Fantasyland rides. We lost money on every one we did. Walt Disney said after it was all over, "How did you boys come out on the rides?" I told him that we lost money. He said, "I don't want you to lose any money on my work, I'll cover your costs." And he did.

The Mad Tea Party ride was another Arrow creation.

Ed: He also said, "We couldn't have done it without you boys. What else can I do for you?" We said, "Nothing, it's just been a pleasure to work with you." But we could of have probably received a concession such as hats or popcorn. They also gave stock at that time because they were broke. We should have taken stock instead of being paid.

We were fortunate that we had really good guys to work with on the Disney side. Bob Gurr's a very clever guy. I have a lot of respect for him, both for his expertise, and as a person. Arnold Lindbergh, he was head of maintenance at Disneyland. I guess actually the head of mechanical maintenance. He's a Swede. Loved to sing, a fine, fine gentleman. Stubborn as a goat, but so were we in many ways. A neat guy to work with. Also Roger Broggie and Joe Fowler and others. Ted Crowell, who supported and worked right with us, particularly on the Small World ride. Vic Greene was an art director. We worked with him a lot. Bruce Bushman was another art director there. We got along well with him. He used to come visit us in Northern California. He and Vic Greene were the guys that you could work with really easily. They'd give you a sketch, and if you say, "Well, that's fine but it leaves a little to the imagination; could you tighten this up a little bit?" or whatever, they were very quick to oblige with no conflicts of any kind.

If you asked Karl if he'd do it again he'd say "NO!" to that.

Karl: Not with what we know now.

Ed: We had an old saying that if we knew what we were getting into we would never have started.

Karl: You bet. When you're young, you go where angels fear to tread.

Dana Morgan, Ed's son, and owner of his own amusement ride manufacturing company, was just a boy during the construction of Disneyland. "I remember that before Disneyland opened, they had the tea party ride at the plant. The building wasn't big enough to build it inside, so they built it outside. At that time, they only had one tea cup on it. I rode it a lot then. I think I was almost certainly the first

The ride that started Arrow's association with Disney; Mr. Toad.

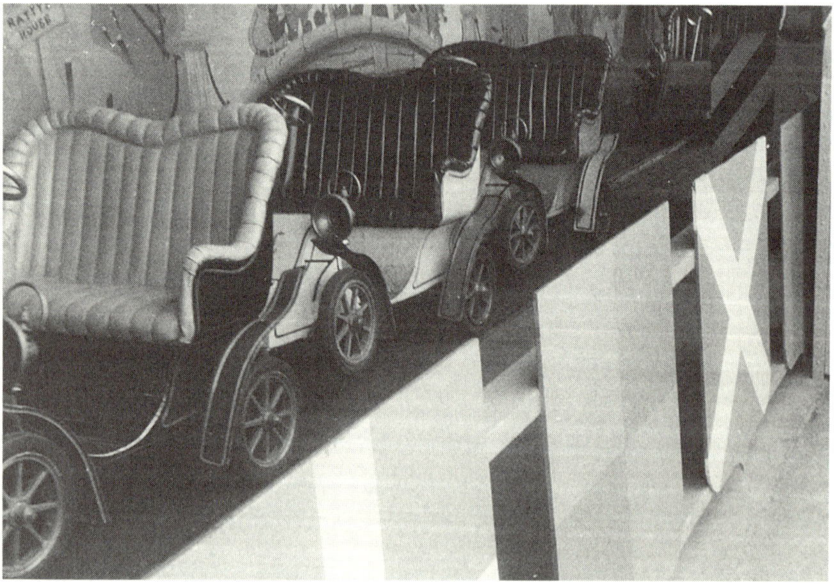

kid to ride it. I was the guinea pig, used to see if a kid was strong enough to turn it, and could stand it without throwing up after riding in it."

"Also, during that time frame, I met Walt Disney. They had set up a test track for the Casey Jr. train, because it was the little train that could. The question was, could it? Could it, in fact, climb the hill? So they actually made a test hill for it to climb. Karl drove the engine himself, and Walt Disney came to see it. I was there that day, and I remember I was impressed, having watched Walt Disney on television, and now, there he was."

"All of those early Disneyland rides were done on very very tight schedules, and very very tight budgets. Totally different from the way Disney works today. That was kind of the key with a lot of that early work at Arrow. It was a different era. We didn't have the design tools that are available to us today. Also, there was no experience at all. All of these ride systems were just totally new and completely different from anything that had been done before. They *were* designed, but they were essentially prototype rides. The reality is that even today, there is still that prototype element to it, although we can design a ride much more precisely today, because of our ability to work in three dimensions on computers."

Disneyland ride systems designed and/or built by Arrow Development.

July 17, 1955	Mad Tea Party
	Snow White's Adventures
	Mr. Toad's Wild Ride
	King Arthur Carrousel
July 31, 1955	Casey Jr. Circus Train
August 16, 1955	Dumbo Flying Elephants
April 23, 1957	Midget Autopia
June 14, 1958	Alice in Wonderland
June 14, 1959	Matterhorn Bobsleds
August 6, 1961	Flying Saucers
1963	Mark VI redesign of Autopias
May 28, 1966	It's a Small World
March 18, 1967	Pirates of the Caribbean
August 5, 1967	Adventure Through Inner Space
August 9, 1969	Haunted Mansion

Also Indian War Canoes, when converted to fiberglass

Two of the most popular attractions of early Disneyland: The Mad Tea Party's Tea Cups and Casey Jr.

HOW TO BUILD A DARK RIDE

Imagine having to build a dark ride system. It had to be quiet, able to take tight turns, reliable and simple to repair, and able to operate fourteen hours a day — every day. A tough job for even the trusty automobile, let alone a system of several dozen vehicles. Ed and Karl met the challenge that Disney handed them and came up with a reliable system that is still in use at Disneyland, more than forty years later.

The Alice in Wonderland ride at Disneyland is a perfect example of this system. This 1958 attraction consists of a number of caterpillar ride vehicles, (the insect, not the company) that progressed down a rabbit hole and into the loopy imagination of Lewis Carroll. The tight curving course required a carriage able to take tight turns, so Karl and Ed devised a tricycle type of tracked vehicle. The two rear wheels would take the weight and propel the car, while the front kept contact with the track. It brought electricity to the rear drive by way of a bus bar attached to the guide rail.

The guide rail itself would be sinuous, while traversing various elevations. Upon exiting the show building, the ride would begin a curving downward progression through a grouping of oversized leaves to the load/unload area. The rail was of a typical small gauge railroad type and would act not only as the guide but also the ground for the system. An electrical bus bar ran along the same course, just to one side of the guide rail, and completed the electrical circuit to power the drive motor. The front carriage ran on two Nylon wheels to

The Alice in Wonderland ride at Disneyland is still as enjoyable today as it was more than forty years ago.

insulate it from the track and provide for a smooth ride. There were also two pairs of side rollers to keep the carriage from falling off the top of the track. Instead of typical upstop wheels such as those used on roller coasters to keep the cars from lifting off the track, Alice cars used side wheels that enlarge as they wrapped underneath the rail flange, thereby keeping the assembly secure to the track. A spur rail brought cars into the service area, where a slot in the rail allowed the nose assembly to be lifted off the rail, and the car removed for maintenance.

A deceptively simple ride at first glance, the tracked vehicles of Alice in Wonderland show the careful planning that must go into even the least exotic of attractions.

The caterpillar vehicles roamed throughout an elaborate multilevel attraction.

Oct. 31, 1961 K. W. BACON ET AL 3,006,286

AMUSEMENT VEHICLE APPARATUS

Filed May 22, 1959 2 Sheets-Sheet 1

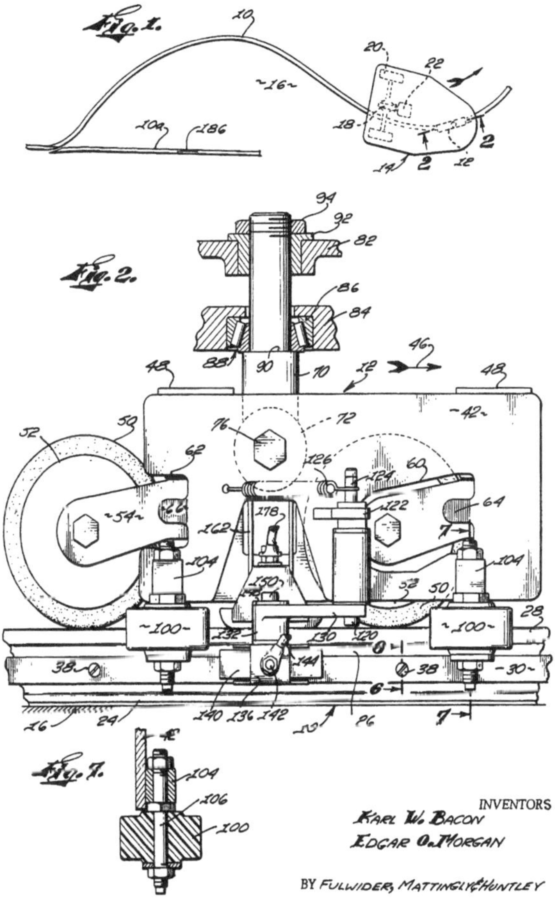

INVENTORS
KARL W. BACON
EDGAR O. MORGAN

BY FULWIDER, MATTINGLY & HUNTLEY

ATTORNEYS

Detail of the nose assembly of the Alice in Wonderland cars.

INVENTING THE MODERN ROLLER COASTER

The first thing a visitor to the Magic Kingdom sees upon approaching the park is a fourteen-story concrete building. The unique aspect of this structure is not the snow on it's upper floors, although for Southern California, it is definitely unusual. The strangest thing is that it does not resemble a building at all. It is in the shape of a mountain, and a recognizable mountain at that, the Matterhorn. This Swiss transplant is a 147-foot portrayal of the famous peak and has been a extremely visible symbol of the park for the last forty years.

Before 1958, the Mountain did not exist, rather just a little dirt mound created from excavations to build Disneyland. Dubbed Snow Mountain, the mound had neither snow nor height, but it did have another sort of high. Bob Gurr relates, "We always had an area in the park east of the castle called Snow Mountain. It was just a lump there. They bulldozed a lot of earth and put a bunch of trees around it. One of the gardeners was growing marijuana up on top, and had been growing it there for about a year before Bill Evans, the landscape architect, went up there. He saw the plants and sent a guy over to the local agricultural office in Anaheim. 'We have these plants. . .' They were removed the next day. So Snow Mountain started out as a marijuana farm."

Walt Disney was in Switzerland for the filming of *Third Man on the Mountain,* and became enchanted with the Matterhorn. He wanted to simulate the breathless race of bobsleds down a curving,

Opposite: The Matterhorn is not only a thrilling ride; it is a beautiful structure. (© Robert Reynolds)

mountainous terrain. The rush was on to complete the replica Mountain by June of 1959. It was part of a redesign of the entire northeast corner of Disneyland and would include the submarine attraction, monorail and autopias.

The mountain would not be just a structure; it would contain two ride systems and also allow passage of the skyway buckets as they journeyed between Tomorrowland and Fantasyland. Walt Disney had seen a Wild Mouse roller coaster in Europe and thought that might be the way to go. A Wild Mouse travels on steel rails, usually angle iron, along a curving route. Unlike today's train configurations, a wild mouse ran individual cars separately along the track. But could it simulate a bobsled? Despite the Disney organizations best efforts, it could not. Something radically different had to be created for such a ride. That is where Ed and Karl came in, and it would change the face of roller coaster design forever.

Karl: About 1957 we had a visit by Admiral Joe Fowler about if we could build the Matterhorn. I'll say that in 1958 we actually started the Matterhorn. They designed the mountain first. We put two tracks in and had to stay in the mountain. We couldn't go outside.

Ed: You bet we couldn't! Essentially they built a steel building, and the steel building was designed, of course, to go in the Matterhorn shape. We had to bridge the distances between the supports they gave us. They gave us a preliminary draft on the building. However, we started to build the ride before they were very far along with the building. They gave us ten months to design the two rides in the mountain.

Karl: So we worked on the layout for the ride. In working on the layout, the goal was to establish the friction slope for the ride, taking into account the various radii, inclines and drops. This was a first for us, and it was a lot of work. We had to miss the other track with proper crossover points. There was not a lot of room for two

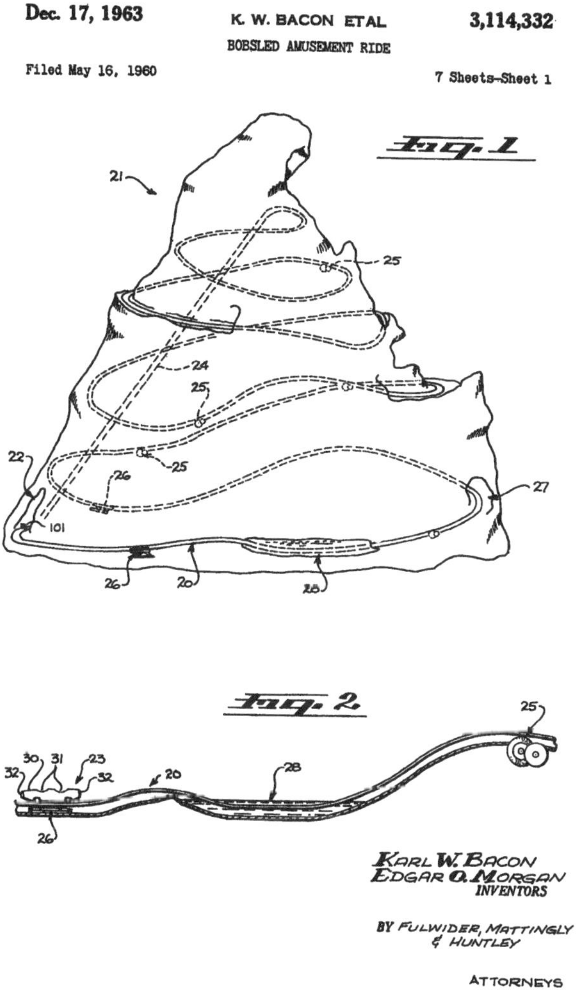

Patent drawing of the ride that would change the history of the roller coaster, the Matterhorn at Disneyland.

tracks. Disney wanted to use angle iron, but with the round pipe you could bend it in any direction.

Ed: What happened, I think, was that WED Enterprises really wanted to be the guys who designed things. They decided that they should design the track and elected to use angle iron. They built a prototype track out of angle iron, and in typical Disney fashion they put it in a beautiful setting. They made a kind of Japanese garden around it. They brought in sand, and raked patterns in it with little walkways.

In the meantime, we had a short little prototype in Mountain View, and we, on the other hand, were just tacking stuff together. If the supports lap each other, so be it, because we're going to wreck it tomorrow anyway, or cut it off and do it some other way. It had maybe sixty feet of track, so we could see the down-travel and an up-section at the far end. We had a squeeze brake to stop the prototype vehicle. And that's all we built.

Anyway, they invited us to come down and look at their prototype. It was an absolute disaster. Joe Fowler was there, and he just looked at us and shook his head. When he got the opportunity, he said, "Don't worry boys the job is yours."

Steel tube rail lends itself much more to accurate bending, because the forces are always the same no matter what axis you bend on. You can't do that with a flat bar, or angle iron, or anything like that. We suspended portable benders on site. The bender had two restraining shoes and a push shoe. It would come forward and bend a little bit. To get the rise, you rotated the bender around the axis of the tube slightly to cause it to rise. Later we became more sophisticated in the bending, and we had what we called a mechanical bulldozer, which is a machine that has a ram that goes back and forth with the shoes on. We had a system where the ram would come forward, still doing incremental bending, but very close increments. On the backstroke, we had a system that moved the rail over and caught it again. That was done by an air-powered motor that we could change the pressure on, thus changing the length of the increment. That gave us the capability of bending big pipe. That machine eventually bent 14-inch pipe. At the time we did the Matterhorn, the question was "Are we able to do this again? Will we do this again?" Besides that, we had only ten months to build the darn, ride and do it however we could.

Eventually we would make a choice between polyurethane and nylon wheels, because we sure weren't going to run steel wheels on a steel rail. The noise being the biggest single factor. We had our necks out a long, long way, because no one had done it before, and DuPont said, "We just don't know." DuPont was the primary supplier of polyurethane at the time. Polyurethane came from Germany as spoils of war after World War II, and DuPont bought the rights from the federal government. Polyurethane rolls with a lot less effort than rubber does. A rubber tire deforms differently and loses more energy to heat than polyurethane. There's a physical and chemical difference that makes it better in that respect. We were conducting tests on small six- or eight-foot long pipe sections. We were loading them and running them twenty-four hours a day. We were doing the same with nylon and other things.

For early tests on the Disneyland site, we were running nylon wheels, but we eventually made the decision for polyurethane, because we had DuPonts assurance, off the record, that they would help us if we got into a real bind. They had a stake in it too. So we went with polyurethane, and eventually, that was the material of choice.

Disney was going to design the sled, but nothing happened. They were just up to their necks on the design of the ride at that time. I decided to go ahead and mock it up so we would have something to work with at least. They said it had to be something like a bobsled, and that's all we got.

I mocked the thing up, and initially I was so concerned with individual dispatch that I felt we should have a safety bumper built into it. So these had very thin fiberglas noses on them filled with foam. If something went wrong with the block system and they tailgated each other, this thing would absorb a lot of energy. We made a lot of drop tests on our prototype, where we dropped and crashed them. It was pretty effective because the nose was two feet long. You can absorb a lot of energy if you have some time to do it. The nose cones were throwaway, because you could mold a new skin quickly, and then just put it in the jig and foam it. The back base that bolted onto the front of the car is reusable, so they just put that

The Matterhorn with the Skyway buckets traveling through the middle. Fitting two separate roller coaster tracks inside the structure proved a complicated endeavour. (© Russell Reynolds)

Dec. 17, 1963 | K. W. BACON ETAL | 3,114,332

BOBSLED AMUSEMENT RIDE

Filed May 16, 1960 | 7 Sheets-Sheet 4

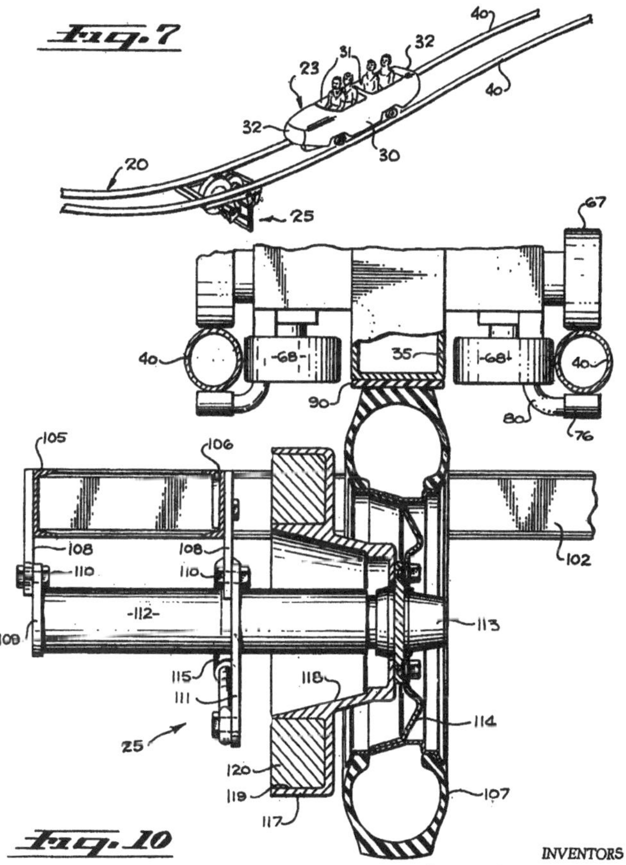

INVENTORS
KARL W. BACON
EDGAR O. MORGAN

BY FULWIDER, MATTINGLY & HUNTLEY
ATTORNEYS

A unique innovation, the booster brake, directly underneath the design that changed roller coaster history, the tubular steel track.

in the foaming fixture and re-foam it. We also had a back bumper made out of a resilient foam cushion with a boot over it. It was probably about six inches thick. Sooner or later you're going to bump into each other, under any circumstance, and you want the best shock absorber that you can get. We wanted to make sure that if they did come together, there wouldn't be any bloody noses.

One criteria we had was that the sled had to be nested by the rails; in effect, we didn't want a Wild Mouse. In a ride such as that, the people are sitting high above the rails. We said that we can't have that; it was not safe if you have a lot of forces that are not controlled. We built the bogies on the sleds so that the rails are at mid-section, and the rails encapsulate the car. So the wheels can fall off entirely if somebody forgot to put in a cotter pin or whatever. There are bars with anti-friction facing on them that will pick up the load and slide, so that no matter what happens, it will still slide down the track. That was a critical feature.

By the time that they could start a bobsled design, the thing had been refined so well, they just accepted it and absorbed it. Nothing was ever said about it. I never actually got anything but a preliminary sketch. The sketch of the sled really didn't show the shape. It was one of the few things we put in Disneyland that was not designed there. I think the only reason the car was accepted is because Walt saw it and liked it. He had the ability to bypass everyone else. Other than that, if you gave it to them for a project you would wait months for sketches. This way we could start making bodies the next day!

Karl: To get enough hourly capacity to be viable, the sleds needed to be dispatched at a fairly close interval. We needed to design a block system to keep them separated.

Ed: The booster is unique to the Matterhorn kind of ride instead of coasters generally, or at least it is more germane and more meaningful there. What it amounts to is, if you take four line-backers and put them in a sled, it might be impossible to squeeze them in, but we could try! In effect, what you are doing is storing a lot more energy, because the energy you store is a function of height and the mass. So whether you like it or not, the sled goes faster than if you have four small people. That was the reason for the equalizing system. What it boiled down to is, we used a very high-grade rubber tire attached to a motor. The tire would contact a platen on the bottom of the sled and boost a slow sled or scrub energy from a fast one. Because the platen on the sled bottom was only five feet long, you couldn't get that much of a bite on it, so the motor came out to about twelve horsepower. You needed twelve horsepower motors at each of these stations, otherwise the sled would overcome the motor. So we said, "Okay, what we have to do is store some energy in the booster." We did that by casting big lead weights inside the wheels. We used those as a flywheel to store energy, and in that way we were able to reduce the motor size to half a horsepower.

On the control board in the control room downstairs, each of those boosters is wired to a meter. So you can see on the meter every time a sled passes over, and you can see if it has a big job scrubbing a lot of energy off, or if there's almost synch as the needle hardly moves and so forth. The operations people scanned that all the time. It tells them a whole lot about what is going on in the ride.

With steel wheels, running on steel rails, rolling friction is almost constant. But in using a resilient wheel, the friction loss rises as the load increases. Tire deflection creates heat and energy radiates to air. So we fooled with densities of the urethane compounds and the thickness of the tread quite a bit, and we found that we could get a little additional performance by having the tire absorb some of the real heavy passenger load. Percentage-wise it was small, but everything helped, because it all comes down to how many people you can get through the station every hour.

We did not use the booster system anywhere else, just out of respect for the Disney people. We didn't feel free to do it, and we didn't want to ask them because we probably would have been turned down! We had people who observed it. We have a lot of sharp people in this industry. They pick up things real quick and get in touch with you and say "I felt this slowing and it wasn't just a friction brake. Or,

I felt this thing being boosted. How did you do that?" And you can't sell it to them.

Karl: We had the idea of running the sled through water to cool it off and knock some of the momentum off. By raising or lowering the water level, we could change the braking effect of the water on the sleds. Walt Disney liked the idea, but then we had the problem of keeping the water out of the bearings and the whole steel rail problem.

Ed: Karl came up with the idea of using water to slow the sled down, but we had pretty much decided not to mention it to the Disney people — to do it in less problematic ways. Then we found out in a meeting that they were going to have a small alpine lake at the bottom. So Karl looked at me, and I looked at Karl. I kind of nodded, so Karl went ahead and told them about our idea. And of course Walt accepts it as a given, "We're going to do it." The problem is not his, it's ours!

The watery splashdown into an alpine lake was Karl's idea. Although it created technical challenges, it proved to be a thrilling ending for the ride.

When installation time came, I was commuting on a regular basis: flying down in the morning, taking the helicopter to the heli-pad, staying with them for the day, and then coming back to the plant. There were changes all along the line in the structure that necessitated some changes in track for us. That's very difficult to do. You can't do it arbitrarily because it upsets the whole thing. In some cases, we made transition fabrications that reached from our track to where it was originally designed for, but were now in different places. We elected then to put rubber bushings at the tie points because we were concerned with temperature variations and the track changing in relation to the building. Also, we were concerned with fatigue failures from deflection.

Labor was the biggest single problem. They all wanted to fight their jurisdictional disputes. "This is our work." The millwrights and the ironworkers were at odds. One thing we did on that ride was use one of the tube rails as an air receiver. A compressor in the basement filled it with air and gave us a constant air pressure for braking throughout the whole ride. Being individual sleds, you had to have a high degree of control as to when and where you slap your brakes on and stop them. The opposite rail was a conduit for all the electricals. That let them run all the electrical service in there for all the blocks. We kept that a secret until we installed it; otherwise the jurisdictional disputes between the trades would have stopped it. The electricians would have wanted to install the track!

Anyway, the track installation was a tough job, but it went well. There were a lot of good competent people on the crews there. Our people watching the installation were communicating with the plant all the time so we could keep things moving. Essentially, it opened on time. We didn't really get the chance to test the whole thing at one time until almost hours before opening.

Karl: I remember when we got part of the Matterhorn finished. Joe Fowler wanted to ride it. We had to stop the car before he got to the end of the track because it wasn't finished.

Ed: It ended sixty feet above the ground! Admiral Fowler got into a sled, and we hoisted it with a big long reach crane and dropped it on the track up there. We had it set up to block and hold it there, and we had a catch device which consisted of sand bags placed on the track on both sides to scrub the energy off. Then we had a squeeze brake right at the last.

Karl: He ran into a sand bag and it would slow him down until he ran into the next one, until he stopped.

Ed: Joe's eyes were as big as dinner plates when he came down! Then the thing stopped and a big grin came back on Joe's face.

Karl: He was pretty scared before he stopped!

Ed: He put on a brave front, but he was looking petrified when he came down.

Joe Fowler also was on hand for another memorable construction moment:

Ed: When the ride was being installed, there's a system for moving cars called transfer tracks. The whole idea was to keep the ride flowing, so we had a system for when the cars come into the station. If somebody's scarf had gotten around a wheel and the car was running slower, you could take the car off by going laterally. It's a real quick operation. You move the track, and another track moves in and lines up perfectly. So with the block system it doesn't slow things down at all. Well, the ride is being installed, and I'm down there. It turns out that somebody in our plant. . .

Karl: . . .forgot that the crush nose on the vehicle made it longer.

Ed: They didn't give them a long enough cut-out in the concrete.

Karl: Joe Fowler was there and said, "Fine bunch of engineers you guys turned out to be!"

Ed: Everybody's standing there, and I look like a horse's ass. So I turn around and bend over and said, "Okay Joe, Give me a good swift kick, and then lets get out the jack hammers and go after this thing!"

Karl: And they did!

Ed: There were jackhammers down there in nothing flat, tearing at the concrete.

There was really a crush to get the Matterhorn open. So I'm down there on site, and this guy under Joe Fowler was assigned the task of having the Disney people work through the night shift, and having supervisors for each trade there. At night it got really cold. You had a plumbing supervisor, a supervisor for the millwrights, and an electrical supervisor. These guys kept coming to me and saying, "You've got to be here all night anyway. Would you mind checking in on my crew from time to time?" Pretty soon, I'm the only guy out there! I'm out there virtually all night. Perhaps around two in the morning I would collapse at the motel, and by six o'clock I'm up again. Every night I had these other crew supervisors, and they're going home to their families, but I couldn't do that. It wasn't a fun time for me at all.

When I saw the ride running for the first time I almost became sick. Because there are two separate rides within the mountain, from a certain perspective, you'd swear that they are on the same track going in opposite directions. Well, common sense tells you that can't be true. That would be a pretty bad mistake! But still, it just got to me. So I went to them and said, "I know you're not going to like this, but can you slow the dispatch down and spread them out a little more until we get a feel for this." I began to feel that we needed increased redundancy in the block system. I communicated this to Karl, and he agreed. Walt Disney was upset because the lines were clear around the mountain twice. He talked to me about it, and I told him my concerns, and he just shook his head and shuffled off. That was it, no further conversation. So we busted our butts to get backup systems on the block braking, so if one sensor failed, another one would pick it up.

All of Hollywood was there, all the movie people. Walt Disney walked down the line and apologized to them, in some cases, telling them that it was going to be a long wait, and taking them out of line. Movie personalities were interspersed throughout the line. One thing they wouldn't do is take those people and give them special treatment ahead of everyone else. They made them go in line, which was right. But he felt so badly about it, he was going to the people he knew and explaining that they were just getting open and didn't want to take a chance on running too many vehicles.

The fact that the Matterhorn is still in place and running after nearly forty years is a testament to the quality of the ride. Bob Gurr mentions that the aged building is under constant maintenance. "I was there on a rainy night and this place leaks like a sieve. Water pours through the place, and it's old wood now, it's sort of like a haunted cavern. Nooks, crannies, stairways, and elevators all over, and when it's running it's really strange. The Matterhorn has to go down often for rehab. It's just a burden, but there's only one Matterhorn ride and people would never allow it to be taken out. All the knowledge that everyone contributed to that thing was an unusual pool of knowledge."

A NEW PARTNER

May 20, 1960, *Film Daily* announced that, "Disney Buys Interest in Outdoor Amusement Firm." That firm was Arrow Development, and the idea for the purchase started a number of years before the event. As early as October 1957, Disney was investigating Arrow and their financial position with an eye to purchase. One aspect that worried the Disney organization was Arrow's financial health. Arrow was the main ride system supplier for Disney; if Arrow did not survive, it would create a vacuum and possibly slow down any Disneyland expansion plans.

By November 7, 1957, letters were traveling between Walter Schulze, the treasurer of Arrow, and Royal Clark, the WED Enterprises treasurer. The offer had yet to be presented to Walt Disney, but Mr. Clark would attempt it when Walt returned from out of town.

Reasons for the purchase firmed up as well, as rumors of the impending purchase of Arrow by C.V. Wood, the flamboyant Texan dealmaker of new amusement park projects, began to worry Disney. The main reasons behind the interest in Arrow:

1. The machine shop at Disneyland had reached capacity, with Roger Broggie's staff working two shifts per day.

2. There was a perceived need for a machine shop close to the Disneyland site, with the presumption that Arrow would build one.

3. By joining with Arrow, Disney would be first in line for new rides and priority manufacturing.

4. Building rides for other parks might be a sound business prospect.

5. Disney would be able to clamp down on the sale of Disneyland type rides to competing parks such as those started by C. V. Wood.

From the Arrow standpoint, a deal with Disney would solve their number one problem: *money*. The difficulty in getting credit had been a hindrance to Arrow, and the Disney name on a loan request would certainly be a help in persuading reluctant bank officers.

Disney seems to have backed off for several years, partially because the machine shop situation settled down and did not seem as critical, and also, a reluctance to become involved in the design of amusement park rides.

All of that changed in 1960, when Walt Disney Productions purchased a third of Arrow Development. That coincided with a move by Arrow to a new 32,500 square foot plant in Mountain View, California. Roy O. Disney stated, "Our purchase of a minority interest in Arrow is a natural development in the close business relationship we have had with them over the past five years. We will license Arrow to manufacture and sell certain engineering and mechanical inventions which we have developed. However, we have no intention of participating actively in Arrow's management or sales organization."

The association would not be long-lasting, ending several years later, but it allowed Arrow to survive and to prosper.

A popular Arrow guide-rail automobile style, the old-time cars can still be found at many parks.

GUIDE-LIMITED AUTOMOBILES

While perhaps not as glamorous as creating the first tubular steel roller coaster, Ed and Karl's invention of the guide-limited automobile ride was equally important to the amusement industry. Before that, most automobile rides at amusement parks had free-running vehicles, limited only by concrete barriers. This presented a situation where accidents and injuries became commonplace.

Disneyland's first Autopia was built with a non-guided system. The Mark One Autopia of opening day featured sturdy cars with stout wraparound bumpers that were maneuverable within the confines of a concrete roadway. Unfortunately the heavy bumpers and unyielding walls often became a source of pain. Ride operators would be caught between the cars and the roadway, suffering broken legs and sprained ankles. Children would hang their hands out of the cars only to find them pressed between the side bumper and the concrete barriers. Also the cars would become wedged between curbs and create the miniature version of a freeway pileup.

At first the Disney staff was hesitant to install the guide-limited ride system proposed by Arrow. They feared that if the control of the automobile were taken away from the driver, the ride would lose its popularity. In order to prove their concept; Ed and Karl opened a center-guide track at Santa Cruz Beach Boardwalk, in Santa Cruz, California. Soon after, Walt Disney arrived in Santa Cruz to inspect the new ride. Apparently, he liked what he saw, because Arrow's guide-limited vehicles became the replacement for the Autopia and also the system of choice for amusement parks throughout the world.

The Midget Autopia of 1957 at Disneyland was a complete Arrow design from start to finish and a favorite with Walt Disney.

Another view of the Midget Autopia at Disneyland.

Ed: We did loads of those center-guided antique cars. I don't know how many installations, maybe thirty or forty.

We did a guided-rail car system for Fantasyland. They saw us running it in other places. The first cars we made were smaller, and we discovered right away that parents were sitting up on the back to ride with their kids, and that was not a good situation. So we made a little larger vehicle. Walt Disney himself saw it and loved it. You just could watch the kids. Kids love automobiles, and although they could not actually steer it, the kids thought they were, and they were grinning from ear to ear. Walt loved it and just ordered it. He said, "I want that ride." So he gave it to his people who did the layouts, and we built the ride for him. It eventually got to the point where dollars prevailed, and it took up so much real estate. They were land poor at this time and didn't have enough land, so it had to be given up. Walt took the ride. He sent it back to us, and we refurbished it, and he sent it to Marceline, Missouri, his home town. He set it up there and set up a fund to maintain it. He insisted on it — he loved that ride. It was one of the few rides at Disneyland that Disney did not design. I designed the vehicle myself, and I made the first plaster of it for the plug and mold.

One fiasco we had was when we came out with the tracked car ride. We had various kinds: little antique cars, modern cars, whatever. We did do portables on those. The track sections were on wood floor sections coupled together, then the guide rail and bus bar on top of that. One of the problems when you install the ride is that installation was always slow, because the track was like a small railroad rail. It was pre-drilled for insulators. But you had to hold the track position, slide the insulator in there, put fasteners through with a counterset head on it, and then put some lock-tight on it so it wouldn't vibrate loose. It was time-consuming. Well, I thought I was a pretty smart guy one day, and I came up with the idea of making an extrusion that had a kind of little section on the back that was like a short tree on a short trunk. Along with that went a rubber part that popped into a hole in the track and wasn't critical for location or anything. It had a kind of button head on it. So you popped that thing in, and then you put the track against it and hit the track, and it jumped into this little rubber tree and locked. It was wonderful!

The Arrow-designed antique automobiles at Knott's Berry Farm. (© Knott's Berry Farm)

We built the first one and put it together in the yard, and we turned the power on to it. A car left the station and ran out of power. Then it knocked the breakers out. So what was wrong? We got our electrical people out there taking voltage readings. The current was going somewhere. It was a low voltage system. What happened was that rubber has carbon in it. Carbon black is where the color comes from, and that is one of the elements that makes rubber wear a long time. So on hundreds of these insulators, the carbon black made them conductors. It conducted the current to ground and it all went away! So you're taking voltage readings, and you start with 24, but then further along you have 22 then 18! The thing won't run, and we're ready to ship. We have done many of them before, but because of my brilliant idea, it's a disaster. We had to quickly have a plastics company make similar parts out of plastic, without the carbon black. So we had to ship the ride without them and quickly air-freight them down there. Fortunately at installation they never knew the difference.

The guided freeway car was where we eliminated, for Disney, all the guys on permanent disability with broken legs and things like that, due to kids corralling them in the station. The guidance system is cushioned, and it's rack and pinion. That gives you a mechanical advantage so it doesn't tend to backspin the wheel as much. The two in combination allow the kids to steer the car about the same amount as with the concrete guideways. Before, they actually hit so hard on the concrete guideways in the same places that in a matter of weeks they could break through the concrete. They were also breaking the vehicles up. Their answer to that was just to keep making the cars bigger until they weighed as much as a full-size automobile. They were just behemoths. If a one-inch diameter tube with a quarter-inch wall was breaking, they'd put one twice that diameter with a half-inch wall in it. Also, in our system when you come into the stations you just split the rail, so there's zero sideways tolerance. The operator has the likelihood of remaining uninjured, and it sped things up quite a bit. Now the operator could step on the running boards as the cars entered the station, and they're already unbuckling safety belts and taking little kid's hands and stuff. Whereas before, they were chasing the cars all over the place.

Probably the most influential designer for the Autopia project was Bob Gurr. Working from the Disney side, he was responsible for designing at least a portion of practically everything that moved at the park. Dana Morgan has strong memories of Bob Gurr visiting the Arrow plant. "Around 1961, Arrow was building the first of their modern freeway cars, as they called them at that point. Bob Gurr from Disney came up, and although it wasn't a Disney project, it was cleared with Disney, and he drew the preliminary layout for that vehicle. I remember being facinated by his ability to just talk with people and have it appear on paper. In a days time he created a set of drawings for what he thought the car should look like. I have one of those cars that I acquired along the way from a client who was taking them out of service. It's still a pretty-good-looking car — sort of the Pontiac or Corvair look of that era. That was a model that they sold to clients other than Disney. The same basic car was built for the Autopia, but they had a specific body on them. Bob Gurr designed the body for them. I was in high school, and I was probably seventeen years old at the time. I was impressed by his ability to bring that about in one day's time."

Bob Gurr recalls, "It was sometime in early 1960, or something like that. Ed flew me up there for the day. Ed's wife took my wife for a day seeing the sights around Palo Alto. Ed, Karl and I were in the shop all day figuring out a new car. The engineers were right there on the shop floor, and I made the drawings right there. We picked out certain car parts; we used 1960 Pontiac tail lights. They had a car that they built for years. I styled it that day. In those days you could engineer and style a car in one day. That was before the guide-limited cars.

"The idea of the cars with the guide solved a big problem at Disneyland, because kids were losing fingers and mashing cars against the curb while sticking their arms out over the side of the bumpers. Just what kids would do. Meantime, the Autopia cars that I was designing were getting bigger and heavier, because I was instituting all the changes that operations wanted. We got to the Mark V car that we called the committee car, because it had all the ideas George Whitney wanted and all the ideas operations wanted, and the car was just too heavy. It started breaking the curbs. In the meantime, Arrow had shifted to the idea of a light car and center-guide steering. So Disney and Arrow had diverged on the idea of how to build a car. "

"There was another car in the interim where we took the existing Mark V body, and we restyled it at Arrow at their new factory in one day. We flew up in the company plane, and I worked with Monty Montellier. I sketched and we bent the shape of the car up with welding rod and masking tape. That's like real wire frame! Monty did a nice job. It was a real hybrid car. I think it was called the Mark VI."

The Mark VI, a light car, started to have problems with breakup too. Bob Gurr, observed the constant welding of the chasis. "It wasn't because this was the first car that we were using that I hadn't designed, and that Arrow designed, it was a case of observation on how a heavy car was worthless and how a lightweight car was worthless. The frame should be flexible. The reason for that is when you calculate a vehicle, you calculate 1g of weight, but actually what happens is, you have a platoon of five cars moving and crashing into another five cars, off center. So you have this big shearing force.

So the idea was to make a car that had a cow-belly frame. In other words, from bumper to bumper was one piece. There were no loose parts, and they could flex, but just slightly — not far enough to fatigue crack."

The Mark VII became the model of choice for the long term. Each car cost over $6,000 and weighed in at a chunky 830 pounds. Over 160 of the Autopia Mark VII vehicles were built for Disneyland. Over time, Dana Morgan has changed his opinion of the vehicles. "It has really proved to be successful, but it is a much more expensive car to build than the Arrow design, or the Morgan design. The Morgan design is more closely aligned with the old Arrow vehicle. At the time, I was fairly critical of the Disney design because I thought it was so complicated and so heavy, but I think that time has proven that it was a better design than some of us thought. Those cars have put on a lot of miles on the road. They are very expensive to build, probably two to three times what we can build cars for, but they've gotten a lot of life cycles out of them, so it may turn out that it was cost effective."

Bob Gurr adds, "In the meantime Arrow built a modification of one of our bodies for awhile. Then we went ahead and made the Mark VII car. It took from 1957 to 1967 to figure out all the ways not to do it. I would never have visualized it when we were designing the Mark VII. If someone had told me to come back in 30 years and these suckers will still be running. . ."

SUBS AND SPACE MONKEYS

Karl: Disneyland was having trouble with their submarine ride going down the track with steel wheels to guide it. So they hired us to build a guidance system.

Ed: Initially, the only work we did on the submarine was some expansion bearings and stuff like that, not bearings within the engine, but to hold the engine in place. Also we fabricated things to do with tying the engine to the propulsion system. Todd Shipbuilding in Long Beach, California, built the submarines. Basically, they did a

The submarines stay on course, courtesy of Arrow Development. (© Robert Reynolds)

good job I think, but Disney may have designed the guidance system. It was a multiple wheel bogie running on a steel track below the water, and it had a big telescopic shaft in the boat so that the boat could rise up and down in relation to the bogie. Well, there were several things wrong with it. Prior to that time, we had developed a really simple system. What we did was put a stem down which was fixed to the hull but was cushioned. One of the ways we cushioned the stem was by using two pneumatic tires with the shaft passing through. By controlling the pressure, you could control the yield and the cushioning. That way, you could control the amount of sway. This gave us a system that you really don't feel. That's particularly necessary on small boats — on the submarine, not so much. On small boats, if you have any rigidity at all, then you are feeling this lurching that we were trying to avoid. What eventually happened is that they were having so much trouble with the guidance system that one day they just shut it down because the boats were coming off the guideway. The telescopic shaft would bind, and it would pull it it right off the guideway, and then the boats would drift into the coral. They would knock out windows and have water pouring into the submarines. The operators were actually trained to throw the round cushions that people sat on into the broken windows, and put their fannies up against it to stop the water flow. There was no pressure because it was just a tiny bit under the water. When Joe Fowler found out about that, he just blew his stack and got us on the phone and said, "Get down here, were going to shut this thing down. We'll call it winter rehab, and by the time it goes back it has to have your guidance system in it." I said, "Joe, there's no point in my coming down. Let them dry-dock the subs and drain out the water; then I'll look and see what they've got and we'll design to suit."

Ed: The submarine ride is, I believe, the largest body of filtered water in the world.

Karl: They have two filters on it.

Ed: And they're automatic. They use a turbidity meter and there are Plexiglas sleeves that the water is being pumped through.

Karl: When it gets dark, it switches the filter on.

Ed: When the water turbidity has risen, it coats the inside of the glass so it shuts that one down and shifts to the other side. Then the operator comes in. The flag is up so they take the cylinder out and clean it and put it back so that it is ready to be shifted back again. I told the Disney people repeatedly over the years, "You guys have a gold mine here. What you need to do is have a backstage tour." People would pay big money to see everything that's behind the scenes. It's really fascinating. The control room on the Matterhorn, for example, is just like being in the control room of a US Submarine. It's just beautiful, all the dials and gauges and everything moving.

Another popular ride from Arrow was based on the Tea Cups of Disneyland. This one is at Knott's Berry Farm, Buena Park, California. (©Knott's Berry Farm)

Karl: During that time we did work for the Navy and NASA. We built the monkey spheres. We had to provide life support systems for the monkeys when they went into space.

Ed: We also had to make the couches for the monkeys to sit on.

The monkey spheres were a contract from Ames Research Center. Their purpose was to send monkeys up in high altitude balloons, as a preparation for sending humans up in similar balloons, and eventually space. Arrow had to create 25 capsules capable of maintaining a safe and, hopefully, comfortable environment for the space monkeys. They also needed to withstand 10g landings and bring the astro-monkeys back safe and sound.

Constructed of foamed fiberglass and capable of holding 100 pounds of equipment, they were packed with environmental units, monitoring equipment and, of course, the monkey. This was 1962, and Arrrow was known primarily as an amusement ride builder. It must have been an interesting change of pace for the Arrow staff.

FREEDOMLAND

Freedomland would become the world's largest theme park for four short years, between 1960 and 1964. It was supposed to eclipse Disneyland, its role model three thousand miles to the West, but this New York park would instead stumble through meager years and ultimately to fall to the World's Fair of 1964/65.

Built at a cost of $65 million dollars, over three times the cost of Disneyland's construction just a decade earlier, Freedomland was designed to accommodate 32,000 guests at a time. Upon its 205 acres you could find pieces of Americana and could look back at such events as the Chicago Fire of 1871. Or you could travel to New Orleans or Old San Francisco by simply walking through the park. But wherever you went in Freedomland, you would be sure to run across rides from Arrow Development. For this new theme park, Ed and Karl provided horse drawn streetcars, a dark ride system, antique automobiles and a dragon called Danny.

Construction started in August of 1959, and continued up until (and beyond) opening on June 19, 1960. While the park initially seemed destined to prosper, a series of misfortunes and miscues would cause Freedomland to declare bankruptcy in late 1964. Plagued by bad planning, terrible location, and ultimately public indifference, Freedomland could not survive.

Ed: A guy named C.V. Wood did the original feasibility study for Disneyland. C.V. was a Texan and a very flamboyant promoter. He and his buddies were working for Stanford Research Institute in Menlo Park. Disney hired them to do a feasibility study for Disneyland. As the result of this study, Disney decided to go ahead and do Disneyland in Anaheim. They sort of took credit for starting Disneyland, an overstatement of their involvement. Everybody wanted to get on the bandwagon in the early days, and these guys were attracting corporate customers like crazy. The thing that C.V. and his associates didn't reckon with was that they didn't have the capabilities of the Disney organization to build a show. They got customers to start these parks, and by and large, most of them failed. We supplied a lot of equipment for parks that went under. The biggest one was Freedomland in New York.

What happened was they built on a former garbage dump. It was poorly planned, and they were working their butts off trying to get this park open. The rains were late; the spring thaw was late. The ground was still frozen. They had a deadline, and the people who put up the money were being pretty tough and hard-nosed about the whole thing. So crews were trying to get blacktop down for parking lots. . .

Karl: In the rain!

Ed: And it's over a mushy base. What happens is, when you start running trucks over it, it was sort of flowing as you went across there. We were going to lunch one day and you could see bedsprings coming up through the blacktop.

Karl: I caught my foot on one!

Ed: Karl went down on his knees because he got hooked on an old bedspring. It was, after all, part of the old dump.

They issued us bicycles because there was so much distance to get around. They gave us these bicycles and told us to use locks and chains or they would be stolen. So we went to lunch one day. We went out to the perimeter of the park and chained them to a couple of trees they had just planted. We came back, and the trees were cut down and the bikes were gone!

Who was the guy that we took to New York with us?

Karl: That was Harold Hodder.

Ed: Harold was probably one of the best welders to ever draw breath. We'd buy a new welding machine and he'd take it all apart. He'd figure that the company didn't know how to make the thing. We had him in New York for Freedomland, and they had given us a new pickup.

Karl, Harold and I went to town one day to buy hardware. Coming back, their planning for traffic was really poor, so they had some bad traffic jams around the park. We came to an intersection and they had a typical New York policeman directing traffic. The cop

An early promotional piece for Danny the Dragon.

turned around and motions to us to move. Harold moves six feet forward and stops. The cop turns around and looks at him. Harold moves another six feet. Pretty soon the cop comes rolling up and starts yelling, "I told you to move up!" Harold replies, "I did move up every time you told me to!"

They also had a lot of trouble with security, so they tightened security way up. They gave us all fancy badges, but Harold would never have his badge on. So, coming through the employee's gate in the morning, Karl and I had our badges on, and he wouldn't have. I could see security looking at him, and he's sliding around trying to avoid them while they're grabbing for him. "You don't have a badge!" and he'd say, "Sure I do, it's right here."

Karl: He kept it in his pocket.

Ed: The people who financed Freedomland lost their shirts. It became a situation where everyone's passing the buck. I'll give an example as to how poorly planned it was. They had these beautiful San Francisco type cable cars. C.V. was able to get art directors to sub out of the studios to do that kind of stuff, but then we did the mechanical stuff. Like for Disney, we'd take the sketches and create it in 3D. C.V. Wood's organization, in my opinion, wasn't sophisticated enough to tie the whole thing together. We built these beautiful streetcars — all oak and scrolled handwork on the edge of the seats — really pretty things. But they didn't get the track in, or should I say, they had the track, but the gauge was wrong. So at the last minute they yanked up some track so the coaches could be sitting there, but they were stationary, they couldn't move.

They opened up the gate and they had this flood of people rush in and jump into the coaches, and they are not going to go anyplace! They kept sitting there and looking around. Finally they talk to each other and decide that it's not going to go anyplace. The harness for the horse is there, but there's no horse. So they get out and go. Then the next rush comes in and fills it up again. They literally almost wore the decks off just getting on and off during the day. There was so much sand left from construction, since the paving wasn't done. People were picking up this sand on their shoes, and when they're shuffling their feet on the cars they were grinding away on the varnished finish.

We also built the Tornado for Freedomland. It was an enclosed ride. Coming out of the station there was a 180-degree-plus turn in it because of some scenic panels. This bulge in the track came back very close to the other section of track. It was not a good thing to do, because if two cars dispatched close to each other, one would hit the other and derail it. But the artists didn't want to move it.

During construction they had a fire in the dark ride. It got so hot that some of the track changed contour. So they hired some people to hammer it back into shape. After that, the ride was so rough they had to have us come back and redo it.

We also did Danny the Dragon. Segments of the dragons' body made up the coaches of the train, and it was guided by a buried cable. The design was used industrially at manufacturing plants, but we found out, that in park conditions, it was not too successful for a number of variables. For one thing, they were always digging, and they would end up with the cable buried at different depths, so you'd have a manual override. There was a radio signal put out by the cable that went to the receiver in Danny, and then to servos that steered the dragon to keep it over the cable. If the cable was too deep, then the receiver lost signal and the operator would have to take over.

THE FLUME RIDE

The water ride has been with the amusement industry for at least one hundred years. One of the most popular attractions of the golden age of amusement parks was the Shoot-the-Chutes. Featuring a steep drop into a large lake, the ride was both simple and thrilling. Passengers climbed up to the loading platform on top of the hill and boarded ten-passenger flat-bottomed boats for the quick decent to the bottom. Once at lake level, the speeding boats skipped over the water like a pebble tossed across the lake, to the delight of rider and spectator alike. All in all, not a bad ride for the late 19th century. It is telling that when Sea Lion Park at Coney Island was demolished to make way for Luna Park, the one ride kept was Shoot-the-Chutes.

Following upon the success of Shoot-the-Chutes was "Mountain Torrent," a 1906 water ride that featured a boat/coaster conveyance that maneuvered through a mountainous terrain to splash down in a alpine lake.

These approaches to handling water for amusement were basically rather simple. At that time, no great amount of research had gone into hydrodynamics, and consequently the full use of the water ride was never explored or exploited, at least not until Karl came on the scene.

Evolving out of the earlier boat rides that Arrow had created, the flume ride took the use of water to new levels. It required a knowl-

Previous page: The Knott's Berry Farm Timber Mountain Log Ride. One of the most popular and most highly themed flume rides, it has entertained guests for over thirty years. (© Knott's Berry Farm)

Shoot-the-Chutes at Luna Park, Coney Island. Even early in the twentieth century, water rides were a popular entertainment. The full ability of such devices was not fully realized until Karl Bacon developed the flume ride, some sixty years later. (Collection of Robert Reynolds)

edge of how water behaved at high speeds and how it could be controlled. Water not properly controlled would lead to all sorts of unexpected and usually unpleasant side effects. To obtain this knowledge, Karl embarked upon what would be the most challenging aspect of his career.

His work payed off, and the flume ride became a staple of amusement parks the world over. From small compact flumes of little over six hundred feet and costing under $400,000, to monsters of over half a mile and, with theming, running into the millions of dollars, the flume ride has been able to take on different personalities and moods, depending upon the installation requirements. Some, such as the Timber Mountain Log Ride at Knott's Berry Farm, take theming to the extreme and present a ride through a scenic mountain log mill and into a forest inhabited by numerous stuffed animals. Other parks have decided upon less theming, allowing the natural scenery and the thrill of the ride itself to be the main attraction. Either way, the ride works on many levels. It was perhaps the first water ride since Shoot-the-Chutes where the spectator had almost as much fun as the participant. Just watching the startled look on the riders as they plunged down the final slope became practically another attraction. A simple ride in concept, a complex ride in reality, the flume ride is one of the great achievements in amusement ride development.

Dana Morgan remembers the flume ride development, "The concept of the flume was really Karl's, and he very much was the one that developed all the water flow information for that. He studied that a lot, and we built a number of test setups. The flume ride was a piece of genius, and the ride has become very much a standard ride. Karl really wrote the book on how to do the water flow. It's again, probably not a dramatic story. It's a hard work story. . . just lots and lots of calculations. So much of what we do creating the rides is just plain old hard work. We have a lot of engineers around here at Morgan Manufacturing with computer screens, and each has a piece of the puzzle. I think, as people observe the design of rides, they expect the design to appear as if there was some magic potion, when in fact, it is just hard work."

The small scale flume was built to study water flow and prove principles.

Karl: About 1962 we started on the flume ride. We had a one foot wide engineered flume. Ed and I were working on the proper friction numbers for the turns and down ramps for the flume. When we got all done we took the lofts and added them up, and we came up with the lofts for the whole ride that way.

Ed: How crude some of the work was. We were building plywood waterways, stuff like that. If the wood runs random for bracing, you let it run random. What we were proving was principles. We didn't care if there were a few leaks. Caulking leaks would have been a waste of time. All we cared about was maintaining the levels of water in the troughs. We were using a scale model, and in water dynamics you are able to extrapolate and blow it up to full scale. We learned an awful lot from the model. Karl, as always, was the theoretician. I helped with the mechanics of the thing, but Karl was out there with his slide rule making all the calculations. He realized right away that there had to be a lot of information on water dynamics, so he started checking and found out that the US Navy was probably the biggest bank of information on water because they were designing ship hulls. They put us on to the fact that water was one of the few areas in dynamics that you *can* work from scale. You can go from little tiny scale up to great big scale, and it still functions. So we were building scale models and grew them up from that. They wouldn't give us a permit for the reservoir that we wanted, so we built a swimming pool! They'd give us a permit for that. We pumped water out of that into a short cycle system so we could prove the principles and solve some of the problems. From this system we built our first ride. Karl, in his usual very accurate and precise way, was setting everything down and retaining it all so you could go to the next stage. Karl had more patience with setting things down in longhand than any person I have known in my life. Just over the period of years he produced volumes of documentation.

Karl: We sold our first ride to Six Flags over Texas.

The prototype flume at the Arrow Development plant. Plywood and leaks, but it proved that the ride was feasible.

Ed: The second went to Cedar Point. They accused us of having taken their ride and given it to Texas, which was not true. Texas had actually put in their order first. We thought everyone understood, as they came in, that was how they were built. But we're still very close friends with Cedar Point people.

Karl: We sold one to Knott's Berry Farm.

Ed: Hurlbut Amusement Company. We sold it to him. He worked as a concessionaire for Knott's.

Karl: The pump at Knott's didn't generate the levels of water that it was supposed to. I couldn't figure it out for a long time.

I put wood in the trough to raise the water level and everything. Come to find out, one of the engineers at the shop had put inhibitor springs on the pump and never told me. I took it off and it worked all right.

Ed: At Knott's, the first guy down the flume was John Wayne and his son. Shortly before that, I was testing it and had ridden it backwards because I wanted to look at stuff behind me, and I hadn't realized that we were coming to the main drop down the chute. When I went, over the top, I thought I had died! The bottom just dropped out from under me. The seat in flume log boats is a

The flume ride worked and proved to be one of the most popular amusement rides of all time. The Hydroflume (following page) was a faster variant of the flume ride. (© Six Flags Magic Mountain)

The prototype flume drop being constructed.

raised section in the middle, and you straddle it. So I'm straddling this thing backwards, and when it went over, the universe just sort of collapsed. Really a surprise!

Dana Morgan recalls that the Knott's Berry Farm log ride was a combination of talents. "Bud Hurlbut and his right hand man, Harry Suker, had very much to do with the Knott's Berry Farm Log Ride. That was an Arrow ride, but those guys did all the theming. That is, in my mind, still probably the best flume ride out there."

He also adds that trial and error went on, even past the opening days of a flume ride. "There was a lot of experimentation with the early rides: the shape of the boat, to get the boat to slow down in the runout but not create too much splash. What we found there was that like any of these attractions, you start from a modest height. The first ones were in the thirty foot tall range. At the time, that seemed pretty exciting to people. But of course, it wasn't long before we were up in the sixty foot tall range, and the business of managing water flow became much more critical. It's just like the coasters — it's an exponential function. The higher you go, your problems are not increased proportionally, they are increased as an exponential factor. If you go ten feet higher, it's a hundred times harder, basically. So we developed the shape at the front of the boat to take the water and turn it around and spray it out the sides low enough so it wouldn't come back on the guests. A lot of work there. There are a few rides out there that have plates on them. They look like race car spoilers. That was when we were still learning, and later we began to incorporate those features into the boats."

Ed: On water flume rides, you can control the amount of splash in what we call the run out section of the flume by using rubber belting of different widths and at different heights. That controls the amount of splash the boat makes when it enters the deeper water of the runout. In Texas, the guy down there said, "I don't want my customers to get wet. You've got to do something about all this water coming into the boats." Karl told them, "Well, you know our

The curved area in the bow of the log was designed to turn water around and force it forward and to the sides. This minimized soaking the passengers but kept enough splash to maintain the excitement of the ride. (© Six Flags Magic Mountain)

experience has been that people love the water." He said, "I don't want water coming into the boats!" So we went to work and raised all the skirting and dried the ride up. The rides popularity dried up. He had to come back and say, "Well, you guys were right." Then we had to change it all back again!

Karl: At Magic Mountain, you and I went out to lunch, and the last thing I said was, "Be sure to open that valve and drain that lower section before you start the ride, because if you don't, it will dissipate all the energy."

Ed: It piled up there then. What do you call that? A hydraulic jump?

Karl: Hydraulic jumps happen when you try to slow it down. If you weren't careful you'd get into a hydraulic jump and lose all that energy.

Theirs lost all the energy. It slowed down from a super-critical flow into sub-critical flow and raised up over the trough and over the plantings.

Ed: A lot of water.

Karl: Forty-thousand gallon pumps.

Ed: Forty-thousand gallons a minute. And it's all going out.

Karl: We came back from lunch and we didn't know. I saw the water all over and knew what they did right away. They failed to open that valve. They didn't think I was serious when I told them about it.

We also had the hydroflume. The hydroflume was faster; it used water at a second stage. That second stage is called super-critical flow. It's a much faster flow. Water flows in two stages, subcritical and super-critical with critical in between. The trough before the station was super-critical when the ride was running. By not draining the water back to the reservoir, the incoming water lost energy and that section went to subcritical and the depth was greater than the trough sides.

Ed: The hull was shaped differently on the hydroflume boats. The front of the hull was substantially different.

Karl: We sold over a hundred-and-some flume rides to various parks in the United States and Europe. We also made portables, but gave it up because the operators were not careful with the water.

We also got the idea of rotating the station about that time. A big turntable. The boat would come in fast to the turntable and then they would load and unload while the turntable went around. They would never stop.

Ed: We did the Hershey Chocolate ride. It was a corporate display ride through the history of the chocolate business. That also used a turntable. The four passenger coaches were supported on a vertical shaft which passed through a slot in the floor. Its lower end attached to a four wheel, electrically driven support vehicle on a bi-rail track. The coaches rotated to maintain the best line of sight for viewing the show. It's a hugely successful thing. We used escalators so you came down into the center of the rotating platform. The people from the perimeter got off in one zone and migrated inward, while others coming down the escalator were going out. So you had all these people turning with this thing and no stopping at all.

Karl has all these terms like laminar-flow, super-flow and hydraulic jump. He had all these nice little water testing devices and I didn't know what the hell he was doing. I was just glad we had someone smart enough who did.

The technologically challenging but extremely popular Flying Saucers in operation at Disneyland

FLYING SAUCERS

One of the most beloved attractions ever to appear at Disneyland was the Flying Saucers of the early 1960's. Basically a high tech bumper car ride, the saucers rode on a cushion of air around a platform, allowing the riders to direct them by shifting their weight. This also allowed the driver to aim for friend and foe alike and create some of the most spectacular collisions this side of the Los Angeles Freeway system.

The overgrown air hockey table that made this ride a reality was one of the more complex and problem-plagued systems that Ed and Karl developed. Made up of over 18,000 individual valves, huge air blowers and movable loading booms, the ride was certainly the most ambitious project of the fledgling Tomorrowland area of the park. Unfortunately, ride capacity versus amount of land used and constant mechanical difficulty doomed the Flying Saucers to a brief life. Opened in December of 1961, they lasted until 1966. The attraction featured a space-age saucer design by Bob Gurr and also an innovative loading boom system that swept the saucers into the loading areas. The saucers were perhaps ahead of their time. Now they remain only as a fond memory and as a reminder that the state-of-the-art attractions that Disney and Arrow strove for at Disneyland sometimes were beyond the grasp of even those capable companies.

Karl: We started on the air ride about 1960. Walt had a prototype unit sent out from the East, and then Ed and I drove it around the shop. The shop was a building with a concrete floor. The

Walt Disney is clearly pleased with the flying saucer prototype. (From left: Dick Nunis, Dick Irvine, Joe Fowler and Walt Disney.)

prototype rattled all its nuts and bolts off and smoked, so we told Walt that this was not for Disneyland. We got the idea of having the air come out of the table.

Ed: They bought the rights for a flying saucer from some character back East and there was nothing unique about it. People had fooled around with it before, but *this* guy just did a real lousy job. Someone in the organization decided it was a wonderful thing, so they sent it out to us, and as Karl said, it shook itself to pieces. We built our own prototype that used a motorcycle engine, and we flew that thing outside the building.

Karl: I knocked down all the carousel horses they had left out for the paint to dry.

Ed: That thing was unbelievable. The building was on a nine-acre site, and Karl was tearing down one side going really, really fast. I thought he was going to kill himself. He kept picking up speed. If it was confined on a table it could never achieve those speeds. But

Karl had his wits about him. Right at the last he reared back, and the exhaust went out the front and it went *'squish'* right down.

But what happened on that concept was that Karl and I had got to thinking. It was a good design, smooth and operated well. There was not a question that it would work. We got to thinking that there was gasoline in each of these vehicles, and also a tremendous air movement. So what would happen is that somehow, no matter how remote, you'd get some gasoline on the floor and it gets touched off by some kind of spark. Then you have a blowtorch because you have this tremendous horsepower. They were like 16 horsepower gasoline engines. It put out a tremendous amount of high velocity air, and for example, you could take a gentle natural gas flame, and hit it with

Karl takes a spin on a piece of plywood.

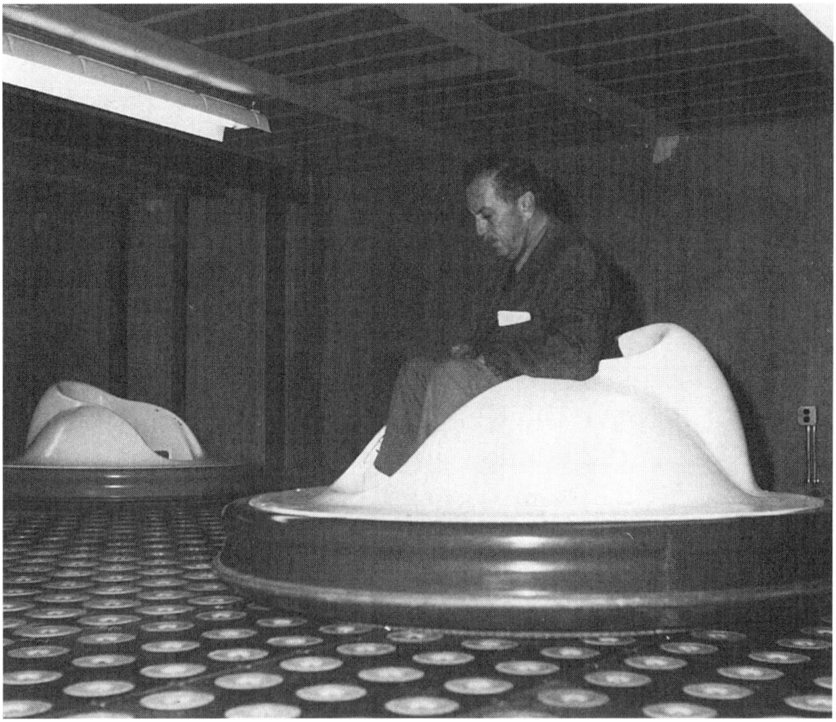

Walt Disney tests the flying saucers at the Arrow Plant.

an air hose, and it becomes a blowtorch. It's really hot. We would have cremated everybody! So we called the Disney people and said, "We don't think we can do it because we've come to this conclusion." They were devastated, but in the meantime Karl had thought more about it. Karl devised a solution to the problem by bringing the air from below. The Disney people asked if we could do it that way. We said we weren't sure but we thought we could. Then the work started in earnest to find a solution to these problems.

Karl: We arrived at 600 electrical horsepower for the table.

Ed: That's right. It was a big ride.

Karl: It was a hundred feet in diameter, fifty feet on a side, and fifteen cars on a side. We had eighteen thousand seven-inch diameter valves. The valves would only open directly underneath the cars.

Ed: That was where the inventing came in! It was a balanced plenum situation. The valves were in balance and the air pressure under the platform kept the valves closed. But once you get air under the saucer, then that air floats the saucer, but it also puts pressure on the valves to pop the valves down. There are a series of gates in the station that you pump a charge of air through. That air goes under the saucers and lifts them and gives them air to counter balance the valves. When you open the gate, they glide out. From that time on, you can see the valves closing right behind the saucers — a little V-pattern, and you could hear them "click, click" closed. So they were open only under the saucers, because if all the valves were open at one time, there's not enough air in the world to keep them up.

Manufacturing a flying saucer.

The Flying Saucers with the Flight to the Moon show building in the background.

Karl: We started up the ride by taking one section at a time and closing the valves.

Ed: What did we call that? Blowing the table? There were a series of galleries underneath the table about eight feet wide. There was a gate that was hydraulically operated at the end of each gallery. In the center is where the air comes down a master tunnel and these other tunnels are parallel. So you're blowing air in from both ends with big centrifugal blowers. Hydraulically, one gate opens, and air goes in there and closes all those valves so you're not wasting air. Then gate number two opens and progressively on down, until the entire table has air under pressure holding the valves closed. The central loading station right next to the center line is an area that you can have open, and you flood it with air to float the saucers, and then they would go out and pick up the table air. To our knowledge, nothing like that had been done before. It was an immensely popular ride.

Karl: It took five minutes to reset the table if needed. The bad part of the whole ride was the fact that we couldn't go above five and one-half inches of water pressure. I wanted to go to six, but the cars would get into a cycle and start going up and down until it threw them so high that the valves would open and the ride would stop. Then they had to reset the table to start all over again. We never really got over that resonation problem. We got Lockheed out for $3,000 a day. I wanted them to search for some solution. All they

Ed takes a saucer out for a spin.

did was give us a report that told us what the problem was, not what to do about it.

Ed: The interesting aspect is that we made a test setup that was not large. In that test setup, the plenum chamber underneath the table was only a foot or so deep. I had the bright idea that when we built the ride, we should build that plenum deep enough so that you could walk around in there for maintenance without running creepers and all the difficulties that went with it. Everybody accepted it. Then we had an immense volume of air and got into this problem, sinusoidal perturbation. Karl, how did we solve that finally? We put dampers on the valves, right?

Karl: We did all we could, but it was never solved to my satisfaction.

Ed: No, we never did get a complete solution, but we made it dramatically better. The original valves had a stainless steel stem and a guide, but they didn't have any damping mechanism on them, because in our tests, there was no need for them. They worked perfectly. But when we had this problem, we designed a dashpot to fix it.

We hired a concern in Los Angeles that moved very quickly to make castings of this dashpot assembly. All 18,000 valves were retrofitted. It didn't take us long because we were able to come up with a design that allowed it to be done quickly. That made a big difference. We know now how to eliminate that problem.

Karl: I remember when we put the new springs in; we had to set them downstairs in the hallway between the two blowers. We would have platforms between two sawhorses that they could work on. The workers would get scared.

Ed: They were worried that the pressure from the blowers would pop everyone's eardrums.

Karl: You go deeper than that when you dive! Once Ed and I were in the ride doing some work on it after 6 p.m. We finally decided that we should go get something to eat, but they locked us in.

Ed: We're in the basement and we are locked in. The air system is going.

Karl: So Ed said that he could boost me up to the air vent, and I could get out and open the gate. Ed pushed me up, and I got in the airstream and went flying off like a cork!

Ed: He literally flew. He just disappeared! Karl always had his pockets filled with data, pencils and stuff. His apron went over his head...

The Flying Saucers at Disneyland. Although enjoying only a brief stay at the park, they are remembered fondly by millions.

Karl: I flew out and hit a bush.

Ed: Those gates or vents were weight-loaded. What they are there for is, if the pressure built up too much, the vents lifted and valved air off. They were automatic controls.

Karl: It was after hours and the ride was shut down, so they were venting all the air.

Ed: Karl took a flying lesson! Another thing happened during installation when we had a crew working down there. All the crew had to wear safety hats. In those days they were aluminum; they looked like a safari hat, but they were aluminum. One of the laborers working down there was a very happy-go-lucky kind of guy. So he was whistling and singing and walking along. Somebody opened one of the gates to charge one of the sections, and *he* disappeared. He went "whoosh," and yelled "Whoa!" His hat was flying along beside him going "clankity, clankity, clank."

Karl: Maintenance didn't realize the pressure or volume of air.

Ed: It's not high pressure but the volume of air coming from a 600 horsepower engine. I looked down there and he was way down at the end. It was kind of bowl-shaped and he's leaning against the concrete. Fortunately it didn't hurt him.

Karl: When we were building the ride, I used a piece of plywood and would float around the table after hours.

Ed: One morning we saw some crates of coke bottles, and Karl and I put the glass bottles around the platforms, and we were flying slaloms through the coke bottles. We were having a ball at six o'clock in the morning!

They keep talking about redoing that ride. We were talking about it this year at the trade show again.

Karl Are they going to wait until I'm dead and gone?

Ed You and me too. I told them a couple of years ago that Karl and I are not getting any younger, and we're the guys who hold the knowledge to bring this thing off. "If you want to do it, do it soon."

MINE TRAIN

The success of Disneyland brought new players into the world of amusement parks. Busch Gardens, Six Flags and numerous others began amassing rides and competing for the tourist dollar. During the early 1960's, the only park with an operating tubular steel roller coaster was Disneyland. For a theme park owner at this time, to be faced not only with the *magic* of Disney storytelling, but also with the popularity of this new roller coaster, was a bit much to swallow. Fortunately, Arrow Development was more than happy to alleviate this last concern. But converting the ride system into a generic roller coaster with a train, instead of individual cars, proved to be a challenge simply because it had never been done before.

Karl was the engineering force behind the creation of the mine train roller coaster, as he explains:

Karl: Six Flags over Texas decided that they needed another ride to spark up the park. Bill Campbell, our salesman at the time, sold them on a mine train ride. Bill didn't know exactly what it consisted of, but we soon developed a system with three trains and three lifts similar to a wooden coaster. I then hired Ron Toomer with the understanding that his tour of duty was for the mine train, and when that was over it depended on our workload.

Ron adds, "In 1965, Arrow Development was in need of a mechanical engineer to help with the development of the Runaway

Train for Six Flags Over Texas. I was hired to fill that slot. At the time I started work, July 1965, the company was testing a prototype section of the Pirates of the Caribbean, and a test track for the monorail system that was installed at Busch Gardens in Van Nuys, California, and Tampa, Florida. My first job was measuring water flows in the pirate ride, and soon after we started development work on the Runaway Train. I worked mostly with Karl since he handled the engineering. Ed took care of manufacturing. Karl was good to work with and was always seeking to learn more about everything."

Karl: Ron and I then went to work on a layout after all site considerations were over, such as location, hills and proximity. Our biggest concern was basic friction slope on various radii, bank angles, velocity, etc. We set up a prototype with a train and took various measurements at different velocities. Nothing worked out until we factored in wind velocity. We then took the information to layout and spent hours on it with a primitive form of a calculator. This was before computers were available. We took track bank angles every

Six Flags Magic Mountain's Mine Train, the Goldrusher, shows off the typical mine train configuration. (© Robert Reynolds)

15-feet. Now a computer can calculate a whole ride in a fraction of the time, while it took us days.

Elaborating upon that, Ron says, "The mine train was a completely new system. We started from scratch on everything. Karl and I learned as we moved ahead, and the ride was running in Texas in less than one year from the start. Along the way we met many things we were unsure of, and each of these was pursued until we had a solution."

"A major item, of course, was the losses due to friction and wind drag, which is critical in the design of any gravity coaster. We spent a great deal of time measuring and debating this issue while we were laying out and designing the course. Late in 1965, and early 1966, we had a test course made up of a lift, and some of the track from the top of the first lift and a train to run around. The train ran the course okay, but in measuring velocities at discrete points on the track, we found that even though the train went around, some of the local velocities were not close enough to what we had predicted. So it was back to the calculations."

"It was always fun when I would tell the young engineers that we had no computers, and all was done with slide rules, math tables and a lot of common sense. Refining of calculations went on over the next five or six runaway trains as we made field measurements of speeds of each of them."

As the ride entered the fabrication phase, the issues only increased. Ron describes an unfortunate turn of events. "During July of 1966 the mine ride was ready to start up, and Karl, Ed and I were on site to get it going. It was hot and humid, and the park was open and teeming with guests. One of the trains was placed on the track at the bottom of the second lift, and preparations were made to send it around to the station. All the principal players from Six Flags were there waiting. The train was pushed up to the lift chain, and away it went. I moved to the bottom of the third lift to await the arrival of the train, which had to pass under the parks railroad track on a tight, climbing curve, to the bottom of the third lift."

The Gold Rusher at Six Flags Magic Mountain still thrills guests more than a quarter century after its introduction. (© Six Flags Magic Mountain)

"All looked good as the first coach appeared under the railroad bridge and into the turn. Then there was a great crashing and banging as the train came to a sudden stop and backed down to come to a stop in the low spot under the railroad track."

"The hitch bars were not long enough to negotiate the tight compound curve, which allowed the coach bodies to contact each other in an accordion like action. There was damage to several of the aluminum castings that make up the coach bodies, and of course, much damage to the Arrow crew! The Six Flags contingent shook their heads and left the scene."

"A fix was easy; a local welder was found and the hitch bars were lengthened. By noon the next day we were ready to go."

Pessimism abounded on the worksite as Karl was soon to find out.

Karl: The Six Flags people had a car in to do the station work. In the layout after the last lift, the track goes through a tunnel and comes up to go into the station. When we finally arrived on site with the rest of the train, one of the workers confided to me that the train would not make it up to the station, as they had to winch the single car to the station every time. The news didn't bother me too much as I remembered the layout back at the plant. The track into the station was on a slope slightly greater than the basic friction slope, so that when a train rose up from the tunnel, the lead cars would pull the last car into the station. So when the first train was dispatched, it was carefully watched by all of the top brass from the office as it came off the last lift, through the tunnel, and up into the station. There was a lot of hand clapping on that run!

We did have our share of problems. One occurred at opening time, when the park manager suggested that I ride the train and check the track coming off of the second lift, which I did. As I came off the lift and around a turn with my rump up in the air, and with both hands holding onto the lap bar, I could see why all the sunglasses and women's handbags were along the fence line! I had a crew out, and we worked at night to calm that one down.

Another was when a train came off the first lift, traveled around a turn, and came to a screeching halt. On examination, it was found that an axle assembly had failed due to poor welds. We located the man responsible and had to fire him. The passengers were not even shaken, due to the design incorporating skid pads. They thought it was part of the ride! Ed and I and crew worked all night on that one.

The Runaway Mine train has been in continuous operation at Six Flags Over Texas since 1966. The tallest lift hill, being only a mere 35 feet tall, may seem a bit quaint today, but the ride still thrills guests and has them lining up for more. The ride started a coaster arms race that continues to this day, with mine trains and their progeny having been installed in practically every park in the world. The Mine Train was a logical evolution of the Matterhorn concept that laid the foundation for all the steel coasters to follow.

NEW YORK WORLD'S FAIR

The New York World's Fair of 1964/65 is probably best remembered as a grand corporate showcase. It reveled in the technological superiority of American Industry and the bright future to come thanks to corporate progress. Not sponsored by the Bureau of International Expositions, and shunned by European countries including the Soviet Union, it had to rely upon U.S. business to create a show. In short, it was the perfect forum for Disney to display and prove its new ride concepts.

The New York World's Fair was a testing ground for technologies that would eventually make their way into Disneyland. One Disney attraction that premiered at the World's Fair was *It's a Small World*. Sponsored by Pepsi Cola, and dedicated to UNICEF, it featured an Arrow Development boat ride through singing animatronic children and dolls. For 95 cents, one could ride along the rivers of the world and see abstract representations of famous landmarks, along with singing children of the world in elaborate regional costumes. It was a captivating show that was brought to Disneyland in 1966. The popularity of the show has stood the test of time, and has since been cloned for Tokyo Disneyland, Walt Disney World and Disneyland Paris. Part of the ambiance of the ride is the gently moving boats that are propelled silently down the waterway. Created by Karl and Ed, the ride system is now in use world-wide.

Postcard view of It's a Small World, the popular Disney attraction at the 1964 World's Fair. (Collection of Robert Reynolds)

Karl: New York was a rough place to work — all kinds of rackets going on. No one would do anything, except for bribes. . .

Ed: . . .From the lowest employee that could impose any kind of restraint on you, up to the head of the building department. The Disney people refused to pay at first. They finally had to give up. Walt Disney said, "This is the last time the Disney organization ever does business in New York City." It didn't turn out to be true, but he was livid. I don't know how much they shook him down for.

I was called in to city hall, and they started giving me the third degree. They asked me about our organization. "Is it a corporation? Where's it incorporated? Who's on your board of directors?" What business is it of theirs? There's a business license involved, and all we want is the business license. We know we have to pay for it. So I finally told the guy who the principals were, and on the board of directors, for example, was Jack Fowle.

"What's his relationship to you?"

"None, he's not a relative or anything."

"Does he get paid?"

"No, he doesn't get paid."

He said, "Nobody works without pay, don't give me that!" This is from the city manager of New York City.

Finally I said, "I don't care what you think; the guy is a wonderful gentleman and a close friend of ours, and he's serving on our board as a favor to us, and that's all there is to it." So finally, they had no choice; they had to give us the license.

I also couldn't believe the workmen. On the Small World ride, I finally made an agreement. There were so many jurisdictional slowdowns that I approached the Disney organization. I said, "I have a plan. All these guys are trying to do is stay on this gravy train with the big wages and overtime. If another trade gets it, they're gone. I have a pretty good group going now; I have ironworkers, millwrights, carpenters, and electricians. If you go along with me, I'd like to offer a deal where we'll guarantee their employment through opening day if they will just not shut us down every time we turn around." So that was agreed on and it worked fairly well. It wasn't perfect; we still had problems.

We had Ted Crowell from Disney working with us. We were very close to Ted. He and Karl worked hand-in-hand making final tests on the water flow for the Small World ride. We were shipping boats from the coast. When the boats came in, we arranged for a little monorail overhead crane system and sling-points on the boats for picking the boats up and taking them in. They weren't going in the water because there wasn't any water yet, so they were storing them there. This went on for a long time, and sometimes it was kind of tough. All the different construction crews that were working didn't pay any attention what we were doing. So they're digging trenches across the track. We would have a boat in a sling, and go around the building and here's a great big trench that you can't get across. You have to make a temporary crossing to get in there.

All during this time the teamsters had a business agent there, and he was logging this activity. At the time the last boat came in, this guy steps up and says, "I declare this as teamsters work." What they wanted to do was collect teamsters wages for teamsters all during the time that these boats were being delivered and shut the job down, of course, because of the jurisdictional thing. It was incredible that these guys could be sneaky enough to be recording every time a boat was delivered. "A boat came in at 6:25 a.m. and was handled by others..."

We also had a problem with the electricians. Opening was coming close, and all the electricians would say is, "We are waiting for the right switches to come in," because the boats were going backwards. Well, with a three-phase current, all you have to do is swap to wires to reverse the direction.

I had one guy that I had an awful time keeping on the job. One of the problems was that their personal appearance meant nothing to them and they didn't spend their money for clothing or anything. They wore the same filthy clothing to work everyday. I had one big Irishman that was a fairly intelligent guy, and if you could get him and hold on to him he could produce some work. On opening day I wondered what to do with him, he was so filthy. I didn't really want him around. So I had this bright idea that I would put him downstairs under the ride, and his job was to go back and walk the trough and make sure there were no leaks. Later, I'm looking for him and looking for him, and I don't find him. Then I hear singing upstairs. He's upstairs on the catwalks, and he just loved to sing, so he was leading community singing by walking backwards on the catwalks on the ride. He'd walk through, then he'd go down and back and come up again and take another group through. "It's a Small World after all... It's a Small Small World!!" I caught up with him and told him for heaven sakes get downstairs and stay downstairs, because if Walt Disney ever saw him dressed that way he wouldn't see the light of day. He was pretty upset about it, but at least I got him down. He had boatloads of them singing like crazy!

IT'S A SMALL WORLD

It's a Small World was one of the great successes of the New York World's Fair. When the fair closed, it was only natural that the ride would be transferred to Disneyland.

The conveyance system itself is deceptively simple. Large flat bottomed boats traverse a course of calm water on a scenic tour at a leisurely pace. But as is usual with most amusement rides, the simplest ride system actually turned out to be among the most complex.

Ed and Karl faced numerous technical challenges with the ride system, and later with its Pirates of the Caribbean offspring. The water control situation had similarities to the flume ride, a challenge already overcome, but the size of the boats and the sheer volume of water created its own unique difficulties.

The boat ride system developed by Ed and Karl went on to great success, not only at Disney parks, but throughout the world.

Ed: We were building a boat ride at Town and Country Village, and at that time we were putting in a ride that was unique to us. Most of the smaller boat rides were circular. The one we built for Santa Cruz was 24 feet in diameter, the boats go around and around in a circle. We wanted something a little further out than that, so this was a ride that was serpentine and went wherever we wanted it to. But this meant propelling the water, and that was a first for boat rides.

The ride was in work, and they were digging trenches and forming for concrete and that sort of stuff, and I was watching the project. We had a tragedy in the family, a nephew killed in a motorcycle accident, so that took me out of the picture, and Karl was on vacation right then. So Walter Schulze stepped in to help watch the contractor. Walt didn't realize that we had to maintain an accurate level, and the parking lot was sloped. So he had guys digging the trenches, but when you fill it with water, it isn't going to be full on the high end! I came back and just couldn't believe it.

Our next foray was a ride called Rub-a-Dub-Dub, from the fairy tale. It went to Elitch Gardens in Denver, and it was the first sale of a commercial ride in which we had the controlled pumping of water to move the vehicles. We used tangential pumps. They were like propeller pumps. Later, we learned to put them in molded wells, and we used submersible pumps for the Small World ride. Those pumps are quite small in diameter, yet you can have lots of horsepower in a small pump because it's submersed. The only thing that

The Small World ride system created by Arrow has been used extensively throughout the world in numerous amusement and theme parks.

Oct. 8, 1968 K. W. BACON ET AL **3,404,635**

BOAT AMUSEMENT RIDE

Filed April 16, 1965 4 Sheets-Sheet 1

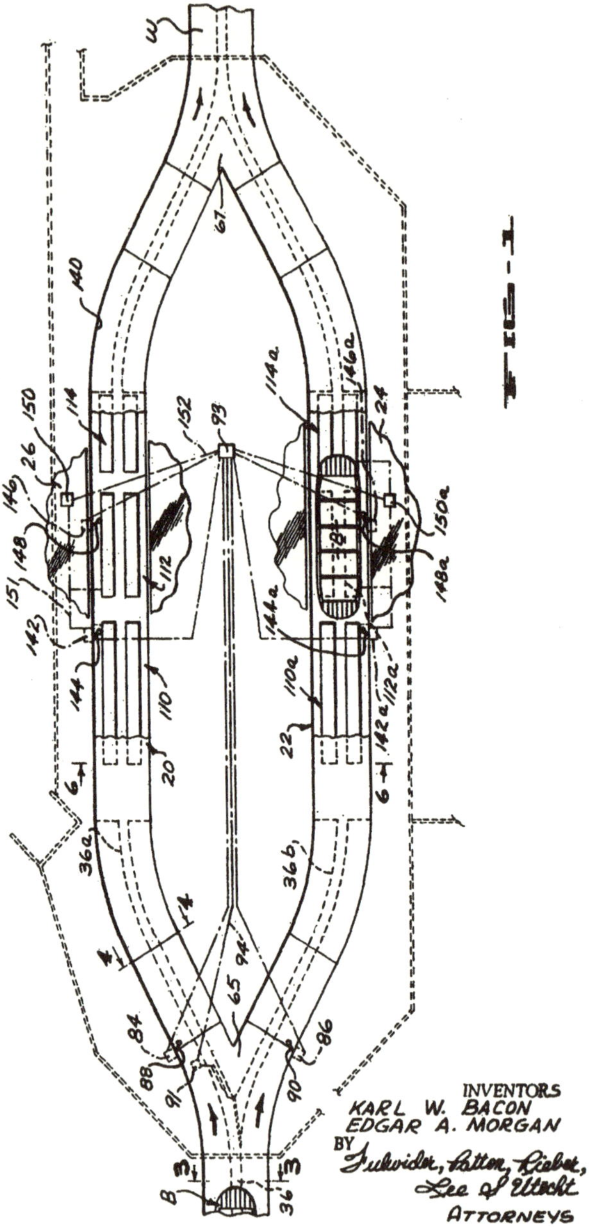

Dual loading platforms, an inventive way to increase capacity.

keeps you from putting more current in the windings is the heat that is generated.

That, of course, went on to be the Small World ride. Many Arrow-developed ride systems were eventually used at Disneyland. Of course the show elements were pure Disney. They founded the theme ride business, no question of that. Nobody in the world can beat them at it. They're just superb at putting on a show. Every boat ride there, and most of the boat rides in the world, carry our system now.

In our system, we just use two side guides, and they are hot dip galvanized because stainless steel is so expensive. The frames are bolted to the concrete base, and the guideways are bolted to the frames, and the wheels simply run between them. They're deep, so as the boat bounces up and down, the wheel just slides up and down in there and its cushioned. You don't feel it. Simplicity in itself. They had an extremely complicated system with all these underwater bearings and everything and massive carriages. We just wiped all that stuff out. Our system has since been picked up and used very widely. On rides like the Pirates of the Caribbean, we used side guides on the boats that were below water, and in that case we had to control the water level pretty exactly. The guides have to go up pretty close to the water surface, yet you don't want the people in the boat to be aware of them. We used cushioned tires underneath on the four

The Small World ride system being tested at the Arrow Development Plant.

Testing the separating mechanism for doubling up the load/unload area, another Arrow creation that sped up load times and increased capacity.

corners of the boat, to guide them. Karl really got into water dynamics and control. He's out there with his little pitot tubes and little vane-type testers that test water velocity. He learned and could talk about laminar flows and all that stuff. He came up with a system of control that was extremely precise.

Small World was at the New York World's Fair of 1964/65; then it came back, and we rehabbed it and installed it at Disneyland. Before it went to New York, we set it up at the shop. All the big redwood timbers we had to ship to New York. The land was settling at the World's Fair site, so it was not possible to use concrete footings. We got redwood sections and built the ride on that. The entire ride was on risers. Every so often inspections had to be done and sections of the trough raised to keep the water flow correct. What happens in the ride is that the water runs down hill about 100 feet to a pumping station, which raises the water level. At each stage between the pumps, the water is flowing down hill. Then at the pump the energy is added and raises the level, but there's enough stored energy in the boat that it crests that little wave — you can't even feel it really — and then it goes downhill to the next pump.

Karl: We had five or six pumping stations. We also had tires in the center of the trough to guide the boats. We used tires to switch the boats from one channel to another. It worked well, you could separate a boat even if it was nose to stern. It *would* separate.

Ed: That was Karl's concept. His idea was to cut the load/ unload time in half. If you bifurcate the track, you are doing two at once instead of one, and it increases the ride capacity dramatically.

There's a little story about Tom Humphries here. When the ride was being set up in New York, we were told that the Disney party was flying up the coast and would be there the next day. The ride was supposed to be operating for them, and satisfy them before it was turned over. We were having all kinds of trouble with unions, and they were stalling, pretending that they didn't have the right relays for the motors, when in fact they were hiding them. We had Tom come out, because he was a very competent person and good with electrical things. Morning came and we were trying to fire the ride up, and everything was backwards. The gate mechanism was not working because they had wired it backwards, and they had done it

The trough for Small World sat upon redwood timbers raised above the concrete floor level.

on purpose so that we would be dependent on them. When Tom arrived, I said, "Tom, here's the hatch. Open the hatch door, go down those steps and see what the problem is." He had his meters and stuff with him. So he started down the hatch to correct this thing. Dick Nunis was there, and Nunis had come ahead of time and didn't know who Tom was. Nunis came on the platform just about that time and he saw this fellow go down the hatch. Nunis reaches down and grabs him by his jacket to haul him back out. Tom sheds his jacket and went right on down! He left Nunis standing there holding his jacket. About three minutes later the wires were switched, and the Disney party arrived and everything worked properly.

At Disneyland there was a UNICEF building right next to the ride. What happened was, there was a bypass channel under the UNICEF building with hatches above that you could lift, and you could see the water flowing. During construction, a crew put on this giant rubber sleeve and didn't tighten the bands on it. So we were flowing water in there, and the sleeve came off and the water flooded the UNICEF building.

Karl: You were underneath trying to put the sleeve back on.

Ed: I was trying to put it on, and the water flow kept increasing until it swept me down the channel.

Karl: I got a piece of plastic and put it over the intake on the pump.

Ed: I thought I was going to drown. I was in this channel moving down underneath, and Karl got some plastic and shut the flow off. I came up through the hatchway, and that's when I found out the UNICEF building was flooded. Stuff like that you have no control over. The guys saw that the bands were on there. They had just slipped everything in place, but nobody had tightened anything. So when the water started flowing the pressure built up, and being

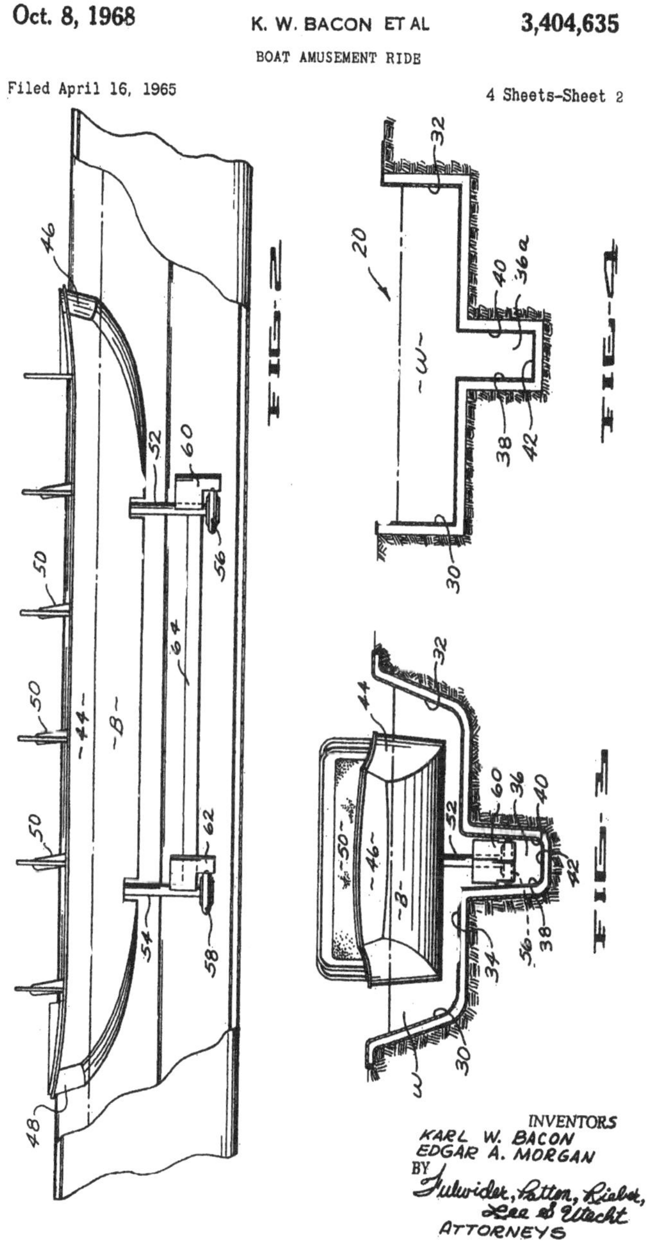

Patent drawing showing the tires running underneath the boats

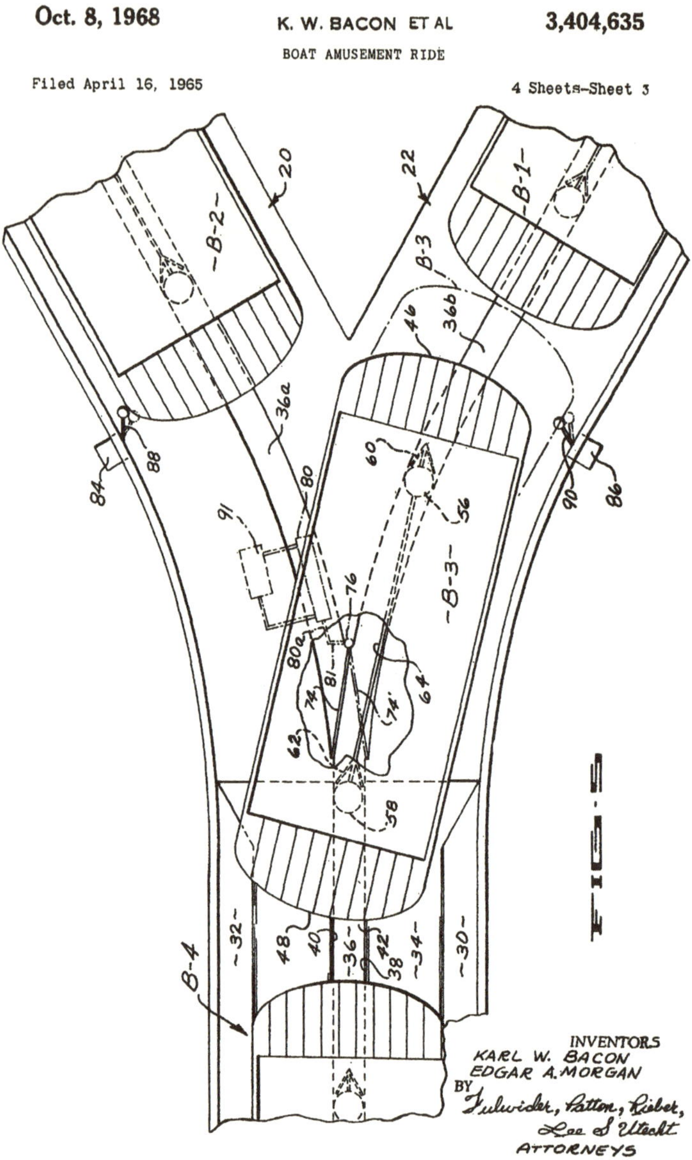

Patent drawing showing how the tires are used to separate boats into different channels.

rubber, they expanded. So when they expanded the sleeve came off and this great big volume of water was shooting down there.

Another instance we had was when we were putting in the ride. There's big bypass channels to take the water through the station while the load/unload is going on. They had large diameter pipe.

Karl: Three foot diameter.

A typical Small World pump sits underneath the trough.

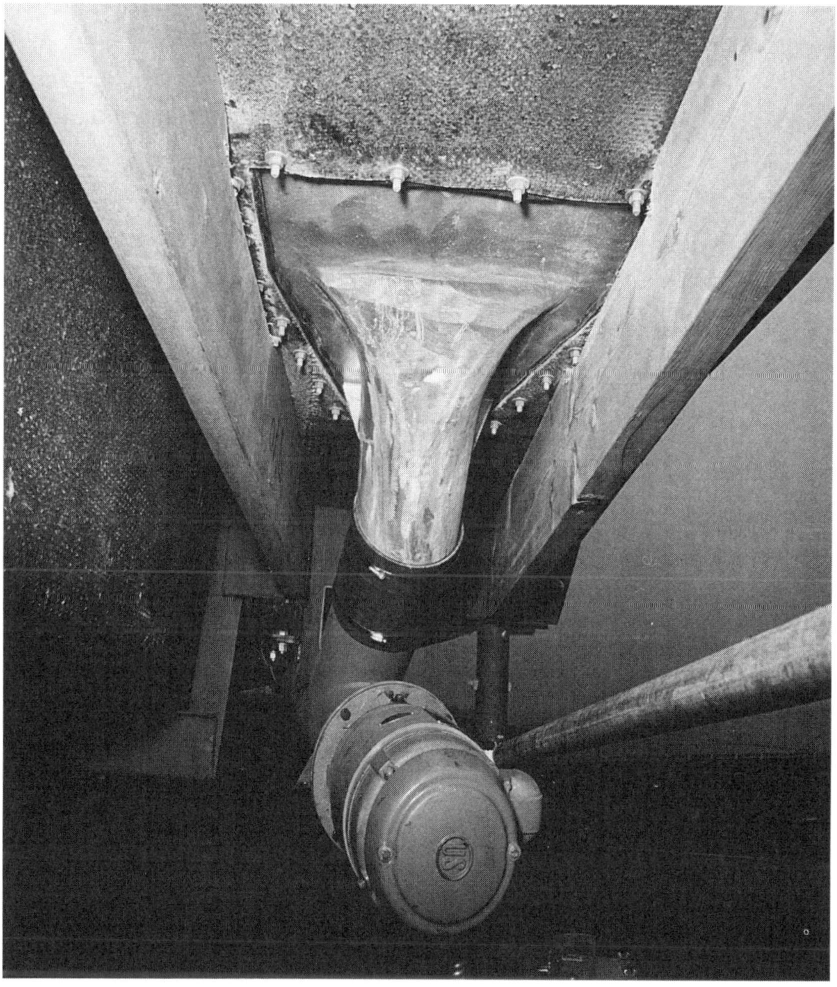

Ed: But they're on an angle, so the connection is an ellipse. They have half-inch thick neoprene gaskets where everything is bolted together. Well, I got a call from Joe Fowler, who said to get our butts down to Disneyland, that we didn't ship the gaskets and it was holding up progress. So I get on an airplane, and then the helicopter to the helipad, and sprint over there and I can't find the gaskets. Our records show that they were shipped. They had building paper on the loading dock to protect it from being scarred up, and I keep feeling a lump there. Finally I get out my knife and cut a slice in the paper, and there are the gaskets! But when I pulled the gaskets out, I found out that the plumbers had seen these big gaskets, and they had been cutting flange gaskets out of them! For the piping, they were useless. I got Hercules Rubber on the line, and had a truck go out to San Francisco to get more rubber and bring it back to the shop so we could cut it and get it on an airplane to Disneyland.

We had a real fiasco on opening day. As usual, the construction of the surrounding area was not finished for the opening of that ride. We had VIP's coming from all over. The whole Disney party had all kinds of people there that they were wining and dining. They were still planting at five or six o'clock in the morning. They were putting in flowers in full bloom — thousands of them. They had been growing hedges in sections in their nursery and pruning them to get just the right shape, so that when they planted them, they'd looked like they've been there forever! We had no chance whatever to really try the ride, but we fired it up and it was working. We were disheveled and tired because we had been up all night for essentially days on end. Finally, about 11 o'clock or so, Karl said, "I've just got to go get something to eat."

"You and me too," I said. So we went to get a bite to eat and a change of clothing. We didn't want anyone to see us now after groveling all night long in water. So we left for a little while, and we got something to eat and changed clothes.

Karl said, "I don't have a cent left, I want to go to the bank." Well there is a bank at Disneyland, so he went. I got back to Small

World first, and I couldn't believe it. The track-way was dry, and the boats were stranded all over the place. There was practically no water in the station at all. Ride operators were running around all over the place. The reservoirs were overflowing.

So the first thing I did was grab the operations manager and said, "Before you do anything else, don't let anyone turn on a valve or switch or anything because there's too many variables, we'll never be able to catch up." They did, and they did a good job of it. They're trained, and they moved quickly and they got things shut off. So I'm starting to sprint from here to there, trying to find the problem. Just

View of the underside of a Small World boat with guide tire in place.

then Karl showed up, and we both saw it at the same time. What happened is that someone had taken a shortcut by jumping across a connecting waterway. There is a main stilling well down there, and the guy landed in the middle of it and crushed it down and just took off. That thing was sending signals like mad and the pumps were reacting. If they had more familiarity with it, they would have realized what was going on and overridden the controls. Instead, they were just draining the ride and filling the reservoir, and carrying people out on their backs from boats since the guests didn't want to get their feet wet. We jumped in there and disconnected the thing and got water pumping again, and about forty-five minutes later we were stabilized and it was running again. That kind of thing makes you wonder why you went into the business!

Our work wasn't all fiasco, just some of it!

PACIFIC OCEAN PARK

Another park that tried to capitalize on the creation of Disneyland, and the theme park revolution was Pacific Ocean Park. Located on a pleasure pier just South of Santa Monica, California, the new park promised rides and exotic locations with an ocean theme. The idea of CBS and the Los Angeles Turf Club, the new park would be located on the site of the old Ocean Park Pier, but with millions of dollars of new investment by corporate sponsors to bring it up to date.

Pacific Ocean Park opened July 28, 1958 to enthusiastic crowds, but after the first year, attendance started to dwindle. Venice, and the surrounding areas were, in the early sixties, already in a state of decline. The area was viewed as unsightly at best, and most likely as dangerous, a stark contrast to the orange groves and strawberry fields of Disneyland's neighborhood. Maintenance at the park began to suffer, and a vicious circle of declining revenues and declining standards continued to plague the park.

An urban renewal project in 1965 cleared out the surrounding area, but also destroyed easy access to the park. The park stumbled on until its 1967 bankruptcy. The following year, rides were auctioned off, but the structures and pier remained until the end of 1973 when it was demolished.

One of the most popular rides at the pier ran on an Arrow Development ride system. Called the Mystery Island Banana Train, it was a small tropical train with bamboo cars that journeyed to the end of the pier and through an elaborate artificial mountain, complete with volcano and earthquake effects.

Ed: What we did was design the coaches of the train to make them look like bamboo. We bought bamboo in San Francisco from importers — all different sizes. We cut them up and made plugs and molds for all fiberglass parts. But when they were colored, they looked like real bamboo. Very effective actually.

Karl: That was another time that the union got into the act. Our crew was carrying a rail up the hill at Pacific Ocean Pier to be installed. The union guy said, "Hold up on that. That's our work!" We could have kissed him, because they were so heavy.

Ed: Going up the hill was heavy and steep, since it was the main lift. This Teamsters business agent shuts everything down. His people were just about ready to kill him because it was blazing hot, and the load was heavier than hell. One of these guys got so mad he started stamping down the plantings. I stopped him. I thought it was going to be a knock-down-drag-out. He was so upset that he walked over to where they had fresh plantings, and this guy was jumping up and down and crushing the plants. I grabbed him by the sleeve and yanked him out of there.

Karl: Remember the wild man who took the train?

Ed: This idiot, without our permission or anything, just took off and tore through the whole ride. The timing was such that he took all the doors that divide the sections right off their mountings. There was a section on that, that had a rotating tunnel. Boy that was effective. We made a big barrel, and it sat on driving rolls like a big tumbler and it had lots of scenes in it with a lot of activity.

Karl: I remember Ed and I coming down the ride late at night, and when we were in the rotating barrel I suddenly had the sensation that we were falling. I yelled at Ed "Something's wrong!" I knew better, but it seemed so real.

Ed: That, by the way, was a steerable train. They had no room to make the turn in the basement, so we built a steerable train that had an antique locomotive on the front of it. You could actually steer the front wheels to go around a corner. Normally the wheels scrub — they stay in a straight line, and the wheels scrub as they go around — but we couldn't do that. The space was so small on this narrow pier that you couldn't turn the train around. Quite a few steerable trains were built later on at other sites that lacked enough room to make normal turns.

At Pacific Ocean Park, another concern was low bidder on the flowing water ride there. They had a different idea. They had all their pumps in one place, and of course that did not work. It pumped the water up to a real high head...

Karl: ...And their boats wouldn't climb the hill.

Ed: They had a lot of egg on their face. Everybody's asking us for help on the thing, and we are not about to help them out at that stage. We couldn't first of all. We had our own hands full since we built the Banana Train there. They went downtown and bought a service station hoist, a hydraulic single-ram, service station hoist. They chopped it down shorter and built a pit, and put this hoist in there. The idea was that you float over top, and they stop the boat, and the hoist lifted you up and you floated away. But what happened is that they had a bunch of movie people out there for the opening ceremonies, and they had been to a dinner and were in formal dress. They had them in a boat, and they missed the timing, tipping the boat over and dunking all these people in their formal attire into four feet of water.

Walt Disney and Joe Fowler (front row) take the plunge on the Pirates of the Caribbean test trough at Arrow Development. A prototype Busch Gardens monorail is seen in the distance.

PIRATES OF THE CARIBBEAN

Opened in 1967, the Pirates of the Caribbean at Disneyland, quickly became the park's most popular attraction, spawning clones in Florida, Paris and Tokyo. One of the most elaborate and technically sophisticated rides ever created, with extremely detailed show elements, Pirates of the Caribbean still maintains the popularity that it had on opening day more than thirty years ago. The show chronicles the working day and hobbies of a band of pirates. Looting a small coastal hamlet, pillaging and plunder, arson and lascivious behavior make a strange story perhaps, for a family attraction, but the subject never seemed to get in the way of the rousing good time that the ride creates.

Part of the allure of the ride is the conveyance method; small, flat-bottomed boats take guests on a cruise that is at one moment peaceful and the next thrilling. From the firefly-lit bayou of Louisiana, to a cave of decaying skeletons, the quiet boats move passengers in a way best suited for a story about a sea-faring people. The ride system that was used was essentially an updated version of the Small World boats. In this case, the fifty boats used side guide rails as opposed to the center guide of Small World. Still powered by water, over 20,000 gallons a minute, the stream could take the 22 passenger boats through the circuit in roughly 15 minutes. In all, over 750,000 gallons of water are stored and moved in order to create the realistic water areas.

The Disneyland ride also included two chutes that propelled the boats down 21-degree slopes to reach the main show area. This allowed the attraction to be built in two show buildings, with the main building outside the berm beyond the railroad tracks. Another feature that was new to this attraction was the uplift. It allowed the boats to rise at a 16-degree angle back up to the load/unload area.

This unique and practical transportation system was designed by — you guessed it — Arrow Development.

Karl: On the Pirates of the Caribbean, they told us what they wanted and left it up to us to engineer it.

Ed: Their biggest requirement was that they wanted it on two levels. That was basically to get it under the railroad tracks because most of the ride is outside the berm.

The Disney party testing the down chute. Walt Disney is in the second to last row.

Going up hill proved to be a challenge as well.

Karl: We had 24 inches of water on the upper floor. The water from the upper floor went down the chute like a waterfall. We had to control the splash at the bottom. So we kept modifying the boat to control the splash. That took a lot of time. We set up a portion of the ride at the plant in order to find the proper nozzle design for minimum loss. Nate Bernstein, an Arrow employee, and I took many readings with pitot tubes before coming up with the best design — lots of time with our shoes and socks off!

The splash would become a major source of grief for those involved with it. Dana recounts his watery adventure: "For Pirates of the Caribbean at Disneyland, we did the boats, down ramps, and all the controls and everything. Also, the guideways, and submersible pumps, and the whole system for that. I was actually working for Disney at that time. I had graduated from college and had gone to work directly for Disney. That was the first job I did there. I worked on commissioning that ride. That was kind of fun because the family built it. So I was on site for the startup process."

"I was twenty-two years old, and right out of college. They gave me a radio and a raincoat, and sent me down into the tunnel to work. There were some problems with it. It's typical of water rides that the guests expect to get a little water on them. They actually *want* to get a little water on themselves. But management wears business suits, and here is a side story that's classic:"

"I was at a flume ride installation at a park, and the general manager came out, and he and two or three people rode the flume in suits. They got their suits wet — very upset. We went in and did a whole bunch of modifications to it, particularly the down chute, and made a dry ride out of it, basically. They opened it to the public, and of course people reached into the water and splashed themselves. So, they called us to come back after it was open and put about 80 percent of the splash back into it. A little of that happened with the Pirates as well. It got to be paranoia about, 'guests-don't-get-wet-at-Disneyland', and after awhile, once we started operating it for the public, it became apparent that people didn't mind getting a little water on themselves. I remember spending several days down in the cave."

Near the end of the attraction, while pirates are shooting at each other and at guests, one of the major effects begin: the boats travel up a waterfall. Being both a way for the boats to get back up to ground level and an exciting climax to the show, it also presented its own headaches.

Ed: The lift was also one of the most difficult things to achieve because no one had done it before.

It turned out that the best way to accomplish the feat was to appropriate roller coaster technology and make it a chain lift similar to a roller coasters lift hill.

Karl: Station dispatch was 6 seconds apart, I think.

Ed: That sounds about right to me.

Walt Disney and Joe Fowler, in the front row, hold on for another drop.

Karl: A hydraulic system operated the boat on load/unload. Each boat was stopped and lifted up on the belt.

Ed: That would stabilize the boat so that it doesn't rock when people are getting in and out of it.

Long hours, spent knee deep in water, have a way of making even the sanest of men act a bit...well, strange:

Ed: I remember Karl and I had been working there on the installation for a long time, and we were in the water quite a bit. There's an area not too far beyond the first big drop. There's a curve in the waterway, and Karl said something like, "You know, why don't we push a boat backwards and see what happens?" We were hidden by the curve and the scenery, so we got down real low at the head of the boat and slowly pushed the boat back upstream. One of the people working there saw it on the monitor and got all excited and said, "My God! Something's gone wrong. The boats are going back up the down chute!"

Karl: Before we installed the Pirate ride we made a setup at the shop. The water was sixteen inches deep. I was in charge of the nozzle design that gives the minimal loss through the pumps. I wore a pair of wading boots and spent hours and hours testing the nozzles in the turns for minimal losses.

Ed: I had forgotten that. They were concerned about having a totally waterproof system with minimal water loss. You couldn't have it going through cracks in the concrete or what have you. We experimented with different coatings. We ended up by bonding 1/16 neoprene to lightweight concrete and had really successful results. We set up portions of the ride at the plant. This gives you some idea as to the complexity of these things. People who ride them don't have a clue as to what it takes to bring it about.

Another example would be when they start up in the morning. There are a lot of boats on that ride, and the boats are stored in a reservoir isolated from the main waterway. When they fire up in the morning, they put a few boats on the line. Those boats get loaded and go down and displace water. As you displace water, your water level rises, so right away your sensors activate in stilling wells. Stilling wells are stainless steel tubes set in the ride at various places that have very sensitive and redundant float systems in them. They tell the system, hey, this water's getting up a little bit — maybe we should peel an eighth of an inch off of it. So the pumps start, and they pump the water from the main trackway into the reservoir, and back and forth. So it's a pretty complex system, but it works extremely well.

That was one of the things we had perfected before it came to Disneyland. Dick Irvine thought that we were going to take that from the Pirates and use it in other people's parks. That's where he had to be disenchanted. They got it from us, and they couldn't keep us from using it somewhere else!

Another time, Don Dreager had been in the East on installations for us. He came back to California the time Pirates was put in.

We were just finishing the setup. There are control gates that keep the water upstairs. During operation, water is going down chutes, and at night you have to stabilize the whole thing and shut the water off going down. You had to stop the upstairs water, or it was all going to be downstairs! We had these control gates that are about seven feet wide. What happened is that we were running the ride and Don had just arrived. They tried a shut down, which would close the gate. The gate locked and didn't close, and now all the water from upstairs is going downstairs. Don didn't hesitate a second. He peeled his jacket off, kicked his shoes off, and dived into the collector box with this rushing water and this big gate, and just disappeared. I thought, oh my God! Don's going to be downstairs! A short while later he pops up. The gate is closed and the problem is over. I couldn't believe the guy.

Karl: Near the end of the ride, the pirates set the town on fire. I remember the head of the fire department coming through the lower doors way down there, and he looked up and saw it and said, "You can't have fire in here!" As he got closer he saw that it was done with colored plastic.

Ed: Mylar. The mylar had gentle fans pushing it with lights on it to refract. It looked like the whole thing was on fire.

Karl: He was going to shut them down.

WALT DISNEY WORLD

Karl: In Orlando we did essentially the same rides that we did in California. When Walt Disney did Disneyland, he got boxed in by the hotels around it, and they couldn't buy more land. When he went to Florida, he got 27,000 acres, so nobody could box him in.

Arrow was asked to reprise their role as the main ride system builder for Disney. The number of attractions that Arrow needed to ready for the 1971 opening of the Magic Kingdom was staggering. They basically had responsibility for every attraction at the new park. Fantasyland, in particular, was dominated by Arrow attractions.

Ed: We didn't do the Peter Pan ride at Disneyland, although people keep trying to give us credit, but we did the one at Walt Disney World. It is an entirely different concept and a lot better system. That one used a combination of a tube and t-bar.

Karl: The t-bar was to take the sway out.

Ed: I was at Disney World a great deal during construction. I remember being there during the Peter Pan installation. We were putting the Peter Pan track in, and I was looking at the drawings and following the track. I looked up and there was a huge air conditioning duct, and I thought, we're going to be running into that thing. So I didn't say anything until I checked it out a little more, and the more I looked, the more certain I was of it. I went to the construction shack and said, "What are your plans there? It looks like that duct is not going to miss." It was a tremendous air conditioning duct, a great big thing. "I don't see anyway you can make a turn of that diameter and not get in the way of the track." And they are shaking their heads no, but about an hour later they are shaking their heads yes.

"It looks like you're right. So what are we going to do?" They said that there was no way that they would be able to change it since they had to tie the whole system in.

I called the plant and said okay we'll bite the bullet and manufacture new track sections. Usually, what you do is, you manufacture and tie one section on, then the next section, but we couldn't do it now. We had to work all from drawings. We had track sections driven down by trucks with sleeper cabs and two drivers, so they are driving all day and night just to get this thing to miss the air conditioning ducts.

We also did the sky ride, all the vehicles. Von Roll, a Swiss company, provided the towers and cableway, but we built all the other stuff. I designed the bucket. It was a stressed skin fiberglass that we delivered to them and they put it on the Swiss system.

Dana also mentions the buckets, "They were basically just a bucket. It was still a Swiss skyway, but we made special buckets for it. Those, I think, were a joint design. Bob Gurr probably did the graphics for the body design and we did the frame design."

Along with the skyway, and Peter Pan, Arrow was responsible for Snow White, Small World, Tea Party, Dumbo, and Mr. Toad in Fantasyland. Dana recalls that, "I think we did the design for the Toad vehicle, but it could have gone either way. Arrow definitely had done the design for Disneyland. That was one of my dad's designs. The original Toad vehicle, which Walt Disney approved, my father made out of sheet metal by hand, himself. Whereas the ones we did for Disney World were fiberglass copies."

Ed: We did the Autopia cars. We did scads of them. We basically duplicated a lot of rides we did at Disneyland, but everything was redesigned. A lot of years had transpired.

Another design of ours was the parking lot trams. We provided the coaches, while the tractors were of Disney design and manufacture, although we provided tractors to many other customers. When we first studied existing equipment we found that not very much attention had been given to safety, braking, accurate tracking and ride quality. Tracking in some cases was so bad that trailer paths could be eight or ten feet inside the path of the tractor.

Working with Tom Humphries we developed trams with four wheel steering, disk brakes and independent suspension. Tracking is so accurate on the Disney trams that coaches follow almost the same path as the tractor, making it possible to "U" turn around traffic islands.

Dana adds, "The Small World ride system was an Arrow design start to finish — water flow and everything. Pirates of the Caribbean was also an Arrow design. The Pirates rides are different, because Disney World doesn't have the drops in it. The original reason for the drops at Disneyland was because the building in California is outside the berm, and the goal was to get underneath the railroad tracks. In Florida, that was not the case. In fact, I'm pretty sure that we used the same boats for Pirates and Small World at Disney World, where at Disneyland, they are clearly two distinctly different systems. Small World has the center guide at Disneyland. The Pirates use side guide boats. I think we used the side guide boats for both attractions in Florida."

Arrow was also responsible for constructing the Omnimover system that was used in the Haunted Mansion and *If you had Wings,* the Eastern airline tribute to flight. For Dana, the Omnimover conveyance was not always a pleasant experience. "They were extremely difficult to make. They were designed primarily at WED, which is now WDI, and Arrow was primarily just a manufacturer of these, although we were involved some in refining it. The Omnimover is constructed with steel pipe rail track located below the artificial floor. The artificial floor is typically three and one-half to four feet above the concrete floor level. A continuous string of vehicles are linked together. They are driven, in this case, by a pinch wheel system. There are fins on all the cars and the pinch wheels drive them. Every 250 feet or so a series of pinch wheels would push the fins. The way we do it now is, we power every third vehicle with an onboard electric motor. I kind of prefer that, but both systems work. The cam path allows the vehicles to rotate. What was unusual about this system, was through a multiplication system, it could turn almost 360 degrees. It could turn clear around. It also had a tipping mechanism in it, so if you went up or down hill, you wouldn't go uphill on an angle. You could tip it so the vehicle was still nominally vertical, or in some cases we would actually profile them to lay back a little bit so they would feel secure, as if they are leaning back in their seat. It was done with two cam paths: one cam for side to side, and a second cam for vertical. This really was a Disney design, and we built these for them and participated in that. It was very successful, with many still operating today. They're a bear to make, and they're very complicated. They are all castings and precision machining. Very expensive."

As complicated as some of the ride systems were, plain old human interaction would sometimes be even more difficult.

Ed: When we first started working with them for Disney World, they sent an army of people to monitor us — because it was so important to maintain schedules or whatever. After awhile, the army keeps getting smaller and smaller and smaller, until we are not noticing anyone, except occasionally Joe Fowler, because they were in it up to here themselves.

Karl: They didn't have time to bother us.

Ed: Which was great! We could work without interference. What happened was, they tried to send Dana down there, and he wouldn't go. What kept him from going, was that he applied at our company, and we hired him. We had a pact that we would not hire relatives, so it was kind of a difficult situation. Particularly for me, because Dana wanted to come to work for us and did not want to go to Florida. But Disney hired a lot of new young engineers because of the scope of the work, and they gave each one a Honda scooter. They had dozens of these kids with these motor bikes. They didn't know what was going on, and they didn't know how to read drawings or anything. We had a guy, Don Dreager, working on the site, who was a real rascal. So Don would set them up. They'd ask questions and he'd give them phony answers. They'd get on there bikes and tear back to construction and get together with their supervisor and tell him all these things they had found out. Of course, that would go to Joe Fowler, and Joe would hold the day's meetings on progress and Joe would say, "Now, I understand that this and that. . ." It turned out that it was not the case, and the kids would be squirming.

Joe had a military jeep, and I'd go down there and Joe would get me into the jeep, and we'd go around in the mud. They'd bring tractors in to drag us out of the mud, and then we'd proceed from station to station. Joe would ask a foreman questions, then he'd say, "Can do boys. Keep up the good work!" And we'd go onto someplace else. I'm looking at this, and things seemed pretty strange to me. So while Joe's talking to these guys, I'm watching them, and I'm finding out that there's cranes picking up steel and they are putting it in one place, and a little while later another crane would come and put it back where it was. They were just making work for themselves. I didn't know what to do; I thought it was ridiculous. We're having a hard time making open, and this stuff is going on. So I finally decide to tell Joe, and Joe looked at me, and he didn't want to accept it.

Dana Morgan was working for Arrow at the time of Walt Disney World's construction. He remembers the support of Joe Fowler in helping Arrow Development do its job. "At Walt Disney World, Arrow enjoyed a trusting relationship with Joe Fowler during the building of the Magic Kingdom. I think it was probably more frustrating to people in their hierarchy. Because on site, there were all these lieutenants and generals that were supposed to be in charge of everything. And the truth was, we didn't play by those rules. If they started to give us trouble, we would just call Joe and say, 'Get these guys off our back,' and five minutes later they were gone. They could end up going to the other end of the park, because he knew that his best chance of getting the rides open was to let us work. We had *all* the major attractions for the park. If we didn't succeed, the park wasn't going to open. And we opened every one of our attractions on opening day. Joe knew that if he would let Arrow have the headroom it needed to do the work, that would be the end result."

Space Mountain was in the design stage as early as 1966, although it would not open at Walt Disney World until 1975. Karl was responsible for profiling the tracks. In the original plan there would have been four separate coasters within the structure. The tracks would also penetrate the building and continue outside the mountain for a portion of the ride.

The lengths of the track would have been:

A Track 2187'
B Track 1845'
C Track 1923'
D Track 1976'

Ed: You finished the design for Space Mountain, didn't you, Karl?

Karl: They decided to do it themselves.

Ed: But actually you did a complete track layout.

Karl: Yes, and part of it was designed to go outside the building, then back in. It was quite difficult with four tracks in the mountain — lots of crossover points plus space for the tracks to miss each other.

Ed: That was the situation when Dick Nunis came to me right after opening and said, "I have to admit that we could not have done this without you. But it's over now. We built this big facility and we're going to do everything ourselves."

They wanted us to build a plant at Disney World, but we refused. Everything was built in Mountain View and shipped. So they built these tremendous, beautiful shops down there. They have a vacuum forming machine that will form a whole twenty-four foot boat in one shot from something like 3/8 inch thick ABS. They can make a whole hull in one shot, and the seat assembly in another, and just put them together. That's the kind of equipment they've got down there. So they said in effect, you guys are through.

Dana adds, "They made it very clear that it was a new era — that they now had all this in-house capability built up, and that they would now do everything themselves. They went through an era where they didn't buy any rides from outsiders at all. They would design and manufacture everything. If you watch their history since then, they've gone back and forth through that cycle several times. They bring it all in-house, then they take it all out-of-house, then they do half-and-half. They're pretty much on an out-of-house cycle right now. That doesn't mean that it will stay that way!"

BUSCH GARDENS

Busch Gardens soon began to seriously compete with Disney for the tourist dollar. Featuring live animals, exotic locals, immaculate parks, helpful employees *and* thrilling rides, the Busch parks grew and prospered. From locations in California (now demolished), Tampa, Florida, and Williamsburg, Virginia, a serious competitor had emerged.

Karl: I almost left out Busch Gardens. We put in a monorail ride in Florida. I think it is the longest monorail ride we'd ever done. It goes through an animal compound.

Ed: That's a very interesting zoo. They use water barriers to restrain the animals, instead of fences. It was enjoyable when we were down there putting it in.

Karl: The monorail at Busch Gardens Tampa was so long we didn't use batteries, we had a power car and a small engine. We put a flume ride into Busch too.

Ed: We also built battery operated boats for Busch Gardens Van Nuys, California.

Karl: They had half-horsepower electric motors in each one, and they'd go all day, 8-10 hours, and be recharged at night. They had 15-20 of them.

Ed: Those were beautiful boats.

Karl: Real quiet. They didn't go real fast, but that wasn't the point.

Ed: The boats were fiberglass, but all the fittings and decks were teakwood, and the seats were plush, upholstered in soft leather with teakwood accents and polished brass. Beautiful boats. They ended up by having a lot of public relations problems from the noise this park created. Finally, Busch closed the park permanently. Those boats were stored under an overcrossing of the freeway when the park closed down. People spotted them and tracked them down, and all the boats were picked up. There are people who love steam launches, and they have little clubs and associations. Once one of these was

The monorial trains in operation at Busch Gardens, Van Nuys, California.

One of the Arrow-built boats for Busch Gardens California. In the background is the park's second Arrow-designed monorail system. This Busch park no longer exists.

converted, they all disappeared, and most of them have been turned into steam launches. They love them because of the low drag hulls.

Karl: Then we did a monorail at Busch Gardens, Van Nuys. It went through the brewery, so you could see how they made beer and the bottling process. It would stop at the various windows so you could look in. I remember the first time they stopped at a window, and you were looking in, and the room just dropped away under you and left you floating in air. The monorail was suspended from above, so it was like going off the edge of a cliff. We had quite a bit of trouble getting that ride operating. The drive mechanism didn't work well, so we had to keep changing it until we got it working.

Ed: There was an operator on each train. For that ride, the prototype we had in the shop was on a very short piece of track, so we never really got to operate it. There were some considerable rises in the actual construction.

The Tampa, Florida, Busch Gardens Skyrail by Arrow allowed scenic views of African animals from a safe and air conditioned vehicle.

But the biggest problem we had with that ride was the contractor. He was given templates for the base concrete work with the great big bolts that hold the base plates down. We discovered that the contractor didn't care — the bolts were not where they belonged. The plates were very precise; the holes for the bolts were exactly the same distance apart. On the site they are all over the place, so we had all kinds of problems. These plates were heavy, so we used helicopters to set the posts.

Karl: The helicopters were double rotor with 5,000 pounds of lift. They had to use them because you couldn't bring heavy equipment into the gardens. They had to hover over and set the columns down. Then the steelworkers would climb up and fasten the bolts for the rail.

Ed: When you're near that thing, it is an exciting piece of machinery. They had a staging area, where the columns were set out ahead of time. They also had some tremendous concrete footings there. They had 8-foot diameter holes with reinforcing bars in them. There was a large digger with a separate hydraulic power source and hydraulic motors on it. They would bring the digger in and drop it and anchor it there, and then the cutter would dig and discharge the dirt. They would then drop the big rebar cages in, and pour concrete to have something to attach the columns to. We got into some pretty interesting things there.

That was also where they made the stone work out of lava stone. They placed all this decorative rock around the gardens, and flooded the boat path. When we came in the next morning, the rock was floating!

The Corkscrew as it appeared at Knott's Berry Farm. This was the first corkscrew roller coaster ever built. It has since been moved to Silverwood Theme Park in Idaho, where it still thrills guests. (© Knott's Berry Farm)

THE RETURN OF THE LOOP

The looping roller coaster is by far not a new phenomenon. Practically as soon as designers developed the gravity ride, others, drawn to the possibilities of the system, started to devise devious and often dangerous methods to increase the thrill.

One of the most ingenious concepts was the vertical loop. Taken from the then popular Loop-the-Loop toys of the early 19th century, where a ball traversed a miniature track system through a loop, the idea was extrapolated into an adult-size version. The first such ride was the Centrifugal Railway of 1846. This Parisian roller coaster featured a vertical loop through a very tight thirteen-foot diameter circle. Then, as today, sandbags were the first riders of this new machine. Although attempts at testing were performed, the coaster lacked such basic and yet-to-be-devised devices as upstop wheels under the carriage to hold the car to the track. Cars and passengers were literally at the mercy of centrifugal force to carry them through the loop. An 1865 clone was quickly closed after a car derailment on its first trip.

The loop idea laid dormant for another fifty years until reappearing in 1895 at Sea Lion Park in Coney Island as the Flip-Flap. The Flip-Flap featured a 25-foot vertical loop that unfortunately was designed as a true circle. Unlike today's loops that most often take the form of an ellipse, the circle put a strain upon the rider's necks, often causing severe injury. This so-called "centrifugal pleasure railway" was anything but a pleasure to ride, and the idea of a looping coaster soon faded back into the mist.

Next up was the Loop the Loop of 1901. This Coney Island landmark, just across the street from what would become Luna Park, was more of a success in that it used the ellipse to send thrill seekers into a whirl. Like the earlier Parisian looping coasters, it too had nothing to keep the car on the track other than centrifugal force. It

The Loop the Loop of Coney Island. After the financial failure of this ride, the loop as a coaster element remained dormant for another seventy years.

also had nothing to keep the riders in the cars. The invention of the over-the-shoulder harness was still a long way off for a looping coaster, waiting for Ed and Karl to come along. Even without such safety measures, the Loop the Loop proved to be a safe ride. It's only handicap was that the four passenger cars created an extremely low passenger capacity per hour — not enough to pay the bills. Even charging spectators admission just to see the ride in operation didn't work. It too, soon succumbed.

The loop seemed doomed as a roller coaster element. It took another seventy years of waiting until Karl Bacon came along to take up the challenge. The return of the loop to popular imagination had begun.

Karl: Ed Morgan, Doc Lemon and I were heading for the airport after finishing with the flume ride at Magic Mountain, north of Los Angeles, when Doc said, "You fellows have finished with the flume and now why don't you do a looping coaster?" It started me thinking about it. I didn't visualize a loop, more like a ride with a long helix — more of a corkscrew. I discussed the matter with Ed and we decided to go ahead with it.

Ron Toomer, a long-time and well-respected member of the Arrow team, adds: "One day in 1970, Karl came back from a trip and he said that while on the airplane he had an idea. He asked, 'Do you think we could make something like this work?' He was moving his hands to describe a twisted shape and I said, 'You mean like a corkscrew? Of course we can.' So started something that has clearly revolutionized the coaster world."

At the time, Arrow Development was owned by Rio Grande Industries the owners of the Denver and Rio Grande Railroad. It was perhaps an awkward time for both Ed and Karl in relating to the company they had built.

Karl: At the time, Ed and I stayed away from the plant in order to give the new president a better chance to operate on his own. I had an office near Woodland, several miles from the main plant, and in it, a large table. I obtained a 12" diameter maple cylinder about 18" long, which I set up on the table. The cylinder became the basis for the engineering project. On it I experimented with different helix angles until I got one that calculated out with the diameter of the ride. I then calculated the velocity through the corkscrew, and at the apex of each loop I held upward force to less than one g-force, just enough to keep the passengers from falling into their safety harness. I also calculated the lead-in curve, both radius and velocity to negotiate the corkscrew. Even down to proper bank angles.

Going back to the toys of the nineteenth century, a model was constructed to show how centrifugal force would keep the cars on the track. Ron was involved in this process, "We started with a small model by forming a helix around a 12-inch diameter pipe and welding small metal ties in place. A small metal car was built, and we invited some park people to see this crude demonstration. We could place small objects in the car to show that they wouldn't fall out. The concept was well received by all that saw it, and most were very excited."

Dana Morgan, who was working with the company at that time, also can attest to the early planning involved in the concept. "The whole process wasn't done like corporate America would do it. There wasn't a big feasibility study. There were discussions at lunch time when Karl said, 'I think we ought to make a coaster go upside down.' And other people said, 'What's in your sandwich?' We're talking 1972 at this time, and that was a pretty far-out thought. I remember he went to prototype, and I was involved with prototype. We took a big piece of pipe, and wrapped some welding rod around it in a big spiral to get the corkscrew shape. We then took it off that big piece of pipe, and Karl had it in his office for awhile as he thought about it and ran calculations. He decided that if you took that shape and pointed it

*The **Steamin' Demon** at **The Great Escape** in Lake George, New York, is another fine example of a traditional Arrow Corkscrew coaster.*

downhill, you could make that work for an attraction, and keep positive g-forces throughout."

"When I was working out in the shop, we had it up on the bench one day, and I went by it and just happened to look inside it. I said, 'You know, there is an incredible television shot here. With the train coming through there, the train is going to be small, and get bigger as it comes at you.' So I went and got Karl, and he looked at that, and I think we began to realize what a powerful experience the thing could be — not only from a ride experience, but also from a visual experience. That has become the standard television shot — more so a few years ago than now. With every new corkscrew, the local TV station had that great shot of the train coming at you. That was one of the things that made that attraction so successful. Not only was it a good ride, but also that *look*. After the quarter scale model ran successfully we made the decision to build it full scale, but not the complete ride."

Karl: After I finished with the model, we went to a full scale version of the ride. We built the corkscrew only, as there was no room for the lead-in curve. So to establish enough velocity for the corkscrew, the lead in track was held high on supports with fifteen feet cantilevered beyond the last support.

Ron remembers the test machine. "In late 1973 a decision was made to go all out on the new product, and a one-quarter scale operating model was built. The original model had only one helix, a chain lift and a four-coach train. Early in the testing we found that axles with single road wheels on each end would not negotiate the tight curves of the corkscrew, and the wheel carrier was born. This has been copied and used by everyone. The other major change was the addition of the second helix, as one did not seem enough."

Dana was fascinated with the new ride, "First, we built just the corkscrew. Then we built a big tower, and a track that came back from the corkscrew and up this big tower. On the other end we just made a turnaround, and we put some brakes, and then we put a lot of sandbags there. We had a winch, and a thing we called a pelican hook, which is a device really from the movie industry — it is a quick release hook. So we would winch the thing backward up the hill, and then we had a way to trip the quick release. But it took almost a day, and the ride lasted probably twenty seconds, and then it would take a day to get the train back up there to try again."

"So we ran it the first time, and it ran really smooth, and this looked really good. So I began talking to Karl about riding it, and he was like, 'No — it's much too early to ride it.' At that time, we did not have accelerometers yet. Today, we would just put an accelerometer on it, and we would know instantly what our true forces were, but at that time we didn't. You have to remember that nobody had ever done this before. Today it doesn't seem very daring, because everybody knows it's no big deal to ride on it, but at the time, it was pretty extreme. I watched, and I knew that the thing wasn't going to hurt you. So I went to the warehouse and got a tire from one of the Autopia type cars, and put the tire in the seat, and winched the train back up again. Karl and I stood under the corkscrew part, and we watched the tire as it went over. You could see the tire just move in the seat, but it didn't fall out. Obviously, it was going to be all right."

"The next day I brought in competition seat belts from a racing car. I brought in shoulder belts and lap belts, and we rigged those up in it. Karl decided, rather nervously, that it would be okay. So Norman Scott and I got in the first seats and strapped ourselves in, and they winched us backward up this thing. We were hanging almost straight down in the harnesses, and the pelican wouldn't release! Finally, I loosened my harness enough that I could see. I got to the point where I'm hanging out of the vehicle so I could see, and I'm yelling down to them because I could see that the cable was hung up. I'm trying to tell them what to do. Right then, it let go. I turned around really quick, and fortunately, from using the competition belts, I knew what to do. I grabbed the belts and pulled them down. I can still remember going through the corkscrew. It was pointing towards the warehouse, giving the impression that the warehouse had turned over twice. I never felt that I had turned upside down. I've ridden it lots of times since then, and I really don't tend to get that same impression now. I don't

CORKSCREW*

Standard Layout
(other variations are available)

Track length 1200 feet

Track Construction: Two 5″ dia. pipe rails on 48″ centers, supported horizontally by a 14″ dia. pipe

Lift Height 70 feet

Lift Power 75 H.P.

Transfer track furnished for storage of one train.

Loading station — By Buyer
(Flush loading preferred)

Vehicles

Two trains (6 coaches each)

Capacity per train 24

Capacity per hour 1400–1600 PPH

NOTE: Exhibit "A" and center line layout available on request.

Overall length 320 feet

Overall width 100 feet

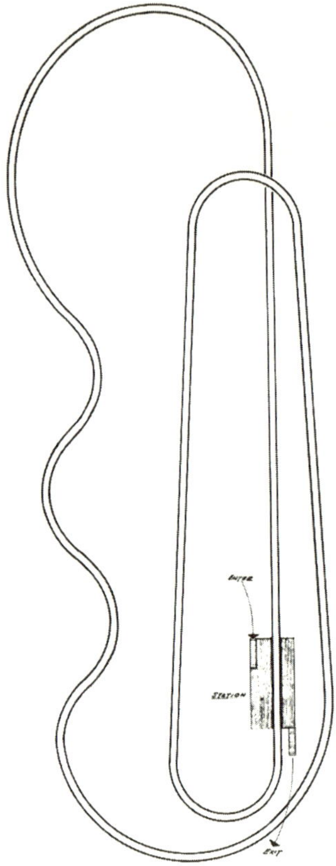

Call or write:

ARROW DEVELOPMENT CO., INC.
1555 Plymouth St.
Mountain View, California 94042
(415) 968-8342

This sales brochure for the Corkscrew shows the standard layout that became extremely popular among amusement parks. Compact, thrilling and visually exciting, this original Corkscrew layout is still in use around the world.

know if it was something funny about the way we had the set up, or no anticipation — then we came to the brakes and just stopped. We were touching the sandbags when we were done. Norm and I got off and said, 'This thing is wonderful! It doesn't hurt you at all, and it's fun.'"

Karl: Terry Brown and I rode it next and had the same problem with the pelican hook, but it went through the corkscrew just fine.

The success of the corkscrew element in keeping riders in their seats by centrifugal forces alone was proven, but few daring riders would venture towards such an attraction if it did not have some form of personal restraint system. That required additional innovations.

Ed: The corkscrew concept, which in effect rotates the coach and its riders 360 degrees around it's longitudinal axis, presented many restraint problems over and above those found in conventional coaches. Our standard practice in design was to try to envision the worst possible scenario or scenarios. The goal is to prevent any undesired occurrences, and in the event that it should happen, the design should contain elements which prevent injury and minimize trauma.

No matter how well the design and manufacture are done, there is always the possibility that a train might stop on the course. The reasons for this could be beyond the manufacturer's control. For example, the rolling friction coefficients can be changed by using a different compound in the polyurethane wheels. Also, different viscosity oil in the wheel hubs, poor track maintenance, shawls, hats and sweaters that become entangled in the rolling elements, high winds, or very low temperatures can also effect the operation.

Regardless of the cause, if a train stops, it could be upside down or somewhere in between. It is obvious that lap bars, no matter how sophisticated, are not adequate. A web strap harness (such as Dana's competition belts) could be effective, but it probably would be slower to load, and puts operators in close contact with riders. The need for upper body restraint, as well as the hips, plus the need for well-padded support to the sides, seemed to favor some type of over the shoulder system. The shape of the bars, padding, strapping, pivot points, locking and release means, all required a great deal of study, prototypes and trials. Since riders vary greatly in shape and size, the restraint needs to be positionable quickly and reliably. In unload mode, the restraints need to be released automatically as the train comes to a stop.

In the history of coasters, there were just a couple of companies doing wooden coasters, and nothing was calculated. They didn't have the know-how to do it. So they built the coaster on site and then they'd try it. If it didn't make the hill — they lowered the hill.

There was an old gentleman, Joe McKee. He was an early coaster builder. I sat with him at Palisades Park in New Jersey, and got to

Patent document showing the Corkscrew.

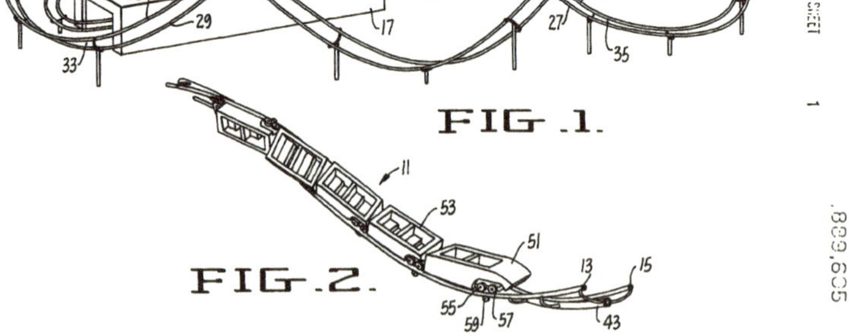

reminiscing about the early days of coasters. They didn't have any upstops at all. They built a coaster for somebody, and the guy spent a lot of money on it and wanted to run it, so they fired it up, and they stood there and you could see lots of daylight under the coaster. They were so frightened by it that they took off and went to a tavern and got stoked because they couldn't watch. Afterward, they staggered back over there and made some modifications on it. You can imagine, no safeties of any kind.

Moving ahead, Arrow Development built a full prototype including lift hill and drop. What made the construction perhaps a bit frightening was the lack of any solid commitments to purchase the ride. Ed gives some indication of this by saying:

ED: It was built on speculation. That's a hard thing to do, because those rides are really expensive. So for small companies to put up a complete ride and then hope that somebody is going to come along and take it off your hands is frightening. It's been known to happen that nobody comes along! Then you have egg on your face and a deficit in the bank.

The fact that the Rio Grande Management was not overly thrilled with the concept didn't help either. Ron Toomer relates: "One day, the then Vice President of Rio Grande Industries (R.G.I.) was out to see the Corkscrew in operation, and he said, 'What makes you think that anyone will ride that thing?' So you see what we were up against. Sometime later the then President of R.G.I. stated that he didn't understand why people go to amusement parks."

Fortunately, amusement park owners did see the value of the Corkscrew. Dana Morgan gives the following details of the first sale: "We got the whole prototype set up, and Marion Knott, of Knott's Berry Farm, came up with her husband to see the ride. She wouldn't ride it. She looked at it and decided not to ride. So he rode it, and he got off and said it was wonderful, and on that basis, they went in the office and bought it. There was no more to it than that. The prototype corkscrew became the Corkscrew for Knott's Berry Farm, and it still exists. It's up at Silverwood in Idaho now. That corkscrew was the prototype that we did all the testing on. We built six corkscrews the next year — a tremendously successful ride. It is still a key element in lots of major rides that havc six or seven inversions in them. They still have corkscrews."

"Knott's was the prototype ride, and probably not the smoothest corkscrew that we've ever built. But still, a pretty good ride. In my mind, those were rides that will always be good rides. By today's standards they are not very big, but still an excellent ride experience. We figured that the corkscrew would be a better ride experience than the vertical loop. You would get two inversions, and it was a better shape. It calculates better, the forces are more even throughout it, and that's still true I think. The elliptical loop is a good element. It works throughout just fine, but I think that the corkscrew is still a purer way to do that. Mathematically, it is a purer way to do it — it's not as intense. And again, that whole process was not driven by an intense amount of decision-making. It was more of a creative process. It was more: this is cool, let's do this; okay that worked, let's try this. You just kind of moved forward."

Karl Bacon and Ed Morgan, together outside of the D. H. Morgan Manufacturing offices. A friendship that has stood the test of time.

PARTNERS

Karl: I remember when Admiral Fowler introduced us to Walt Disney for the first time. He said, "I want you to meet these boys with their suits on, because you'll never see that again."

Ed: My wife loves Pendleton shirts, so I was wearing Pendleton shirts before they became expensive.

Karl: We had a fellow named Bill Campbell in sales. He went out to Japan and sold an Arrow ride over there. One of the Japanese executives came over to our plant to look at it and meet Ed and I. Later he said to Bill, "In our area, the heads of the company wear neckties." Bill explained to him that in this country, if you get successful and build something up, you don't want to dress up. You come to work in the same way you always did.

Ed: I was in Atlanta at a convention helping Dana out. I was helping Dana set the booth up. So I was there at the booth, and a small party came along with a young woman, mid-thirties or so — that's young as far as I'm concerned. She left her little party and came over to me. She asked, "Are you Ed Morgan?"

I said, "Yes, I guess I must plead guilty."

And she said, "You're not wearing a necktie?"

I looked back and replied, "Well, no. I'm not a necktie kind of person."

She said, "Well, you don't even have a business suit on."

"Well," I said, "I guess I'm guilty there too." She walked back and talked to her people and she's shaking her head. As she walked away, I said, "What you see is what you get!"

Ed: We tend to take employees for granted. In the heat of the moment, the goal is to get the work done. When the plant closes down and people are not around anymore it just hits you that they were a pretty unusual bunch of guys. And I'm not talking just about engineers, accountants and sales people. I'm thinking of people like Les Phelps and Paul Harvey. Les Phelps was a guy who was always there. He did everything. When needed, he would be on the assembly crew, but he was more of a yard person than anything else. Paul Harvey was in charge of mechanical maintenance at the plant. We had a lot of vehicles. We had everything from Cushman scooters to big diesel trucks. Les Phelps was pretty much in control of the yard. And the yard was a big function. We had a system at the plant where we had bunkers in a field of five acres. We had bunkers that had water, natural gas and electricity, both single and three-phase. These bunkers had lids on them, so anywhere you went, you had utilities close to you. We were digging up the yard often, putting footings in, so you couldn't pave the yard. It was crushed base rock, graded to drain. The bunkers made it possible to do all this work. Les would be taking care of hoses and extension cords, just a myriad of jobs. If you have someone that does it automatically and intuitively, you get so used to it just happening that you don't realize how important they were. Of course artistic and creative people such as Dave Willis and Monty Montellier were instrumental in putting the icing on the cake.

I am well aware that any success I may have achieved would not have been possible without the support and help from my family, my business associates and the best crew ever put together. The fact that Karl and I worked together for thirty years and are still the closest of friends speaks volumes. I can't imagine anyone having better luck than I have.

Ed, with part of his extensive collection of antique cars. A recently restored Bugatti convertible (not shown) won its class at Pebble Beach Concour. Karl's hobby is building complex grandfather clocks, from design and parts creation to completion.

Karl: I would say that whatever success I may have gained is partly due to my wife Jane, and to my two children, Susan and Nancy. My wife, who stayed at home with the kids, and in later years worked in a flower shop as a designer. I love them all very much.

Karl: We sold the business about 1973.

Ed: Then, we had contracts as consultants. That went on about five years. It was supposed to be five years, but what happened, as far as I was concerned, is that I submitted a lot of things. They asked me to submit ride ideas, and I submitted quite a few things. It wasn't going very well for me. One of the things I submitted was called a giant swing. They turned it down flat, saying that it was not practical. As you know, the Germans finally came out with it, and now they are all over the place.

The next one was the Jumping Jack. Because they wanted a small ride that was inexpensive for parks that couldn't afford the big stuff. So we developed that over a really short time. We had Jumping Jacks out on the columns. I made a study of the air cushions and so forth. It worked fine. I pointed out in my proposal that you could use them singly, back to back or side by side. It was patron-operated; you just start moving up and down, and you get into a harmonic and just keep going. We were jumping so high we were just about to hit our heads on twenty-foot-high ceiling. I pointed out further that you could make them radial, and rotate them while they jumped. Well, Arrow decided that was the way they were going to do it. They prototyped the thing and spent a pile of money doing it, and everything got so heavy that the passengers couldn't bounce them. Then they came up with a system where all the passenger was doing was tripping switches in the floors and the Jumping Jacks were powered. After $150,000 dollars, or whatever, they scrapped the whole thing.

Another one was the Racing Derby. There was once a ride called the Racing Derby. It was really an attractive ride, and a couple of them existed in this country. I made a study of that ride, and got under it at Cedar Point and looked at it. It was a maze of cables and grease. So I had the idea of changing the design entirely and getting away from the cable drive system. I was using a sine wave track, but being driven from the center. They prototyped it up to the point where we were going to try a horse on it for the first time, and I went in to check it out. They had a torch cutting it apart.

I told them I didn't want five years, I wanted out NOW! They said, "well, stay a little longer." I stayed as a consultant for another six months or so. I was having guilt feelings because I wasn't putting anything out. They let me off. Karl stayed the full five years.

Ed and his son Dana about 1986, with one of the Morgan trains for The Grizzly.

LASTING MEMORIES

What follows is an interview with Dana Morgan, at his D. H. Morgan Manufacturing plant in La Selva Beach, California. Dana's broad background in the amusement business covers over 40 years. Being the son of Ed Morgan, he grew up in the business, and as a child was more than happy to volunteer his services as a tester of new ride systems such as the Tea Cups, and the Matterhorn Bobsleds. Later, at age 14, Dana was a ride operator at an Arrow-owned kiddieland in Palo Alto, California.

After graduating from Cal Poly, Dana went to work for Disney and started his career by helping to prepare the Pirates of the Caribbean for its 1967 opening. Not wanting to move to Florida for the Walt Disney World project, Dana instead became an employee of Arrow Development and worked with his father and Karl on many of the new rides under development.

Dana moved on to become the General Manager of the Santa Cruz Beach Boardwalk, a position that still brings back fond memories for him. It was only the opportunity to become the president of Arrow, under the Arrow/Huss banner, that brought him back to manufacturing. It soon became apparent that no matter how successful Arrow would become, the parent company was dragging them quickly into bankruptcy. It was at that point that Dana started his own company, D. H. Morgan Manufacturing.

Morgan Manufacturing has quickly grown from a small carousel manufacturer into one of the world's premier roller coaster design companies. With a string of 200 foot high Morgan coasters dotting the American landscape, Dana has repeated the success of his father and Karl. While technology has changed considerably, Dana and his wife Paula are the first to admit that without Ed and Karl, the modern amusement park would not exist the way we know it today.

Dana: When you grow up in the business, I'm not sure that it ever really dawns on you that you're doing something unusual. It's like, that is what your family does. I was born in 1944, and they started the company in 1946, so obviously, I did not have any comprehension.

One of the earliest things I remember fairly clearly is being at the plant in Mountain View. I used to enjoy the guy that painted carousel horses. My mom would take me to watch that. I have a photograph as a six- or eight-year-old watching him do that. As I got a little older, I particularly enjoyed watching the prototype shop, the creative part of the work. As a little guy, you don't understand the engineering work as early as you do watching the one-offs, or what we call the prototypes.

The other one that I recollect was the Matterhorn. The Disney people wanted to build it on angle iron rail, and dad and Karl wanted to build it on pipe rail. That clearly was a significant moment in time for roller coasters — that decision to go to round pipe rail. It might have happened somewhere later anyhow, but clearly, that was where it happened; there's no question about that. Arrow had built a test track at the end of the yard, at the old Moffitt Blvd. plant, and I was the first kid to ever ride the test setup. So I wasn't the first adult to ever ride the Matterhorn test, but I was the first kid to ever ride it. That was a fun coaster ride.

I don't remember Disneyland's construction as a particularly hectic time. But then again, in this business, there is probably no time that isn't a hectic period. It's the same at Morgan Manufacturing. I've been doing this thirty years of my adult life and been around it fifty years, so I don't remember the Disney time being any different.

I do remember Disney World, and at that time, I was working for Arrow, and that was probably a bigger push because we did more work there. We did fourteen rides for Disney World, and we were actually working, at one point, with three shifts around the clock. We did all the Fantasyland stuff, Dumbo, Small World. We did several Omnimover projects for them, we did the Sky Buckets, and we did the Autopia cars. We also did Peter Pan, all the dark rides, Pirates, parking lot trams. That was probably the busiest that Arrow ever was, because we also had some work for other clients in that same time frame. Our facilities were really taxed.

Organizationally, on the technical side, usually my dad was the one that would do the communications. Karl preferred not to be in that, although he would do it when he needed to. Karl was

Paula and Dana Morgan (front row) and Laura Keller (wife of Dan Keller, General Manager of Worlds of Fun) and Steve Okamoto (Chief Coaster Designer for Morgan Manufacturing) (second row) prepare to take a ride on Mamba, the 200-foot-tall Morgan coaster at Worlds of Fun. (Photo by Lee Schwabe)

usually working ahead of the stream. He would be working on the advanced stuff. My father would be working on the things that needed to ship right now. So again, they had a pretty good relationship that way. It was a very hands on kind of business. Even when the company had 220 employees, they were still *very much* involved. One of the things that typified that and kind of explains the change after they sold the company: In the main plant in Mountain View, the offices were in the front part of the main production building. My dad and Karl had offices next to each other, but their offices had two doors on them. One door opened into the hallway of the office complex, but the other door opened directly into the shop. You knew that at any moment one of those doors might fly open, and they came out there, and you were doing something wrong, they would know it because they both had x-ray vision!

Originally there were four partners, and then that changed to three partners — two of which were original partners. They sold to the Denver and Rio Grande Railroad in 1972 or '73, right about there. The Rio Grande Industries people came in and sat us all down, and said that nothing's going to change — its going to be just like it always was. Bud Dreager took me aside and said, "Don't believe a word they said. I've been through three or four of these. *Everything's* going to change." *They* believed what they said to us. They just didn't understand the nature of the company. Fine people. People of good integrity and high intentions. I'm sure if you asked them today, they would say, "We just didn't understand those guys." Arrow was a California company, and the cultures were just different — the way the people think in the workplace, and even though it was early in the Silicon Valley days, that whole different way of working had started to happen. For guys in Denver running a railroad, that just made no sense whatsoever. I didn't even realize how conservative Denver was. They were very straightforward — again, very fine people, but just a no-risk-taking environment.

With the transition to RGI, the company began to lose it's creativity, really, within the first couple of years of ownership. A lot of the creative people began to leave. Karl and my father were still

Construction of Mamba at Worlds of Fun. Two hundred foot high roller coasters, such as this one by D. H. Morgan Manufacturing, exist today due to the innovations of Karl Bacon and Ed Morgan nearly forty years earlier. (© Worlds of Fun)

working on a contract basis at that time. The classic story there is, dad and Karl invented the river raft ride long before anybody built it. RGI wouldn't let them build it. They said there wasn't enough equipment to sell, because all the work was going to be done in concrete, and the only thing you could build was the lift and station and boats — there wasn't enough profit in it. We built a model and everything, but the RGI people stifled it.

The swinging pirate ship — my father had that all drawn up long before anyone ever built it. RGI didn't think it was a good idea. The pirate ship, if they let us go forward, that could have been patented. That swinging element at that time was not a known element.

So that's where the company changed. They maintained their ability to fabricate high quality attractions, and they maintained their ability to design from their standard package.

The relationship that Dad and Karl had was unique. Karl tended to be more the theoretical guy, and dad was the guy who got it done. But they worked very closely together, because they had a tremendous respect for each other. When it comes to taking credit for a particular part, they will probably each try to give the other one the credit for it. It's fun to watch them. They have never been the ones to upstage each other, because they have a lot of respect for each other. Basically, Karl would be in his office running numbers, and my dad would be much more in the shop making sure that we could get it built.

It was interesting when Karl was here a few months ago. I wanted to show him how we are designing coasters now, in 3D on the computer. So Steve Okamoto, who is our chief coaster designer, set up some drawings on his computer for Karl to look at. Steve apprenticed under Karl, and that's where Steve really learned his trade, originally. We just meant for him to see it casually, because he just had a serious stroke. Karl was probably eight feet back from the computer monitor, and we're explaining it to him a little bit. He walked that wheel chair right up to the screen, and kind of pushed everyone else out of the way and started asking very technical questions. I think that went on for forty-five minutes, and he finally said,

"Oh, I wish we had this. What we could have done if we had this tool." Then he kind of thought about it and said, "Well, you're doing it. We could have gone two hundred feet high." The only reason we can do it today is because of the work that Karl and others like him did back then. Computers just allow us to look at it in a lot more detail. He was fascinated, but also frustrated that he had missed that window, that he hadn't been able to design with that equipment, because he would have been able to make a computer sing.

EPILOGUE

*Ed Morgan accepting the **Hall of Fame Living Legends** award at the 1998 International Association of Amusement Parks and Attractions (IAAPA) trade show. Flanked by his family, Ed accepted, on behalf of himself and Karl Bacon, the award for lifetime achievement in the amusement industry.*

The Hall of Fame award is presented each year at the International Association of Amusement Parks and Attractions (IAAPA) trade show. Its purpose is to honor those people who have made lasting contributions to the development of the industry. Throughout the years, the list of honorees has been a who's who of pioneers in the business of fun. Past inductees have included Walt Disney; Walter Knott, founder of Knott's Berry Farm; roller coaster pioneer, La Marcus Thompson; Ferris wheel inventor, George Ferris and Steeplechase park owner George Tilyou to name just a few.

Ed Morgan and Karl Bacon became **Hall of Fame Living Legends** at the 80th annual IAAPA trade show in Dallas, Texas on November, 1998. Karl and Ed accepted the award jointly via video tape and Ed Morgan accepted the award in person. Fittingly, for the two partners that have shared most of their working careers together, this was the first time that the award was shared by two recipients.

The unsuspecting author riding one of Ed and Karl's creations, the Tea Cups. Little did he know that many years later he would be writing about the creators of this and many other Disneyland ride systems. (© Russell Reynolds)